Introduction to
the World Economy

BY

A. J. BROWN

M.A., D.PHIL

Professor of Economics in the
University of Leeds
Sometime Fellow of All Souls
College, Oxford

Ruskin House

GEORGE ALLEN & UNWIN LTD

MUSEUM STREET LONDON

FIRST PUBLISHED IN 1959

*Printed in Great Britain
in 10pt. Times type
by C. Tinling & Co. Ltd.
Liverpool, London and Prescot*

Introduction to the World Economy

PREFACE

THE aim of this book is to introduce readers to some of the salient features and problems of the world economy and to give some indication of the main ways in which economists set about the task of analysing them. No previous knowledge of any branch of economics is assumed, and it therefore becomes necessary to devote some space—the first three chapters, in fact—to a general account of what economies are, how they work, and what terms and concepts are necessary for the rest of the discussion. I have tried here, and throughout, to avoid technicalities, especially monetary technicalities, as far as possible.

After the first three chapters, the book proceeds to discuss, with as much reference as possible to the broad statistical facts, why the world economy is as we find it in a number of respects; why productivity varies from one community to another; how prices are formed; how productivity and prices determine the livings which communities and families get; how national economies have grown, and continue to grow; what determines an economy's occupational structure (apart from local specialization); how local specialization comes about; how the pattern of international trade has grown and changed; what are the main sources of insecurity in economic life. In conclusion, the ways in which international institutions have grown, and may grow, to deal with some of the problems which emerge are briefly discussed.

I have tried, in short, to provide some background of economic fact and analysis against which current events—especially in the international field—and, for that matter, some of the matters normally dealt with by students of history or geography may, I hope, be seen to rather better advantage. I am acutely aware that to apply even the simplest economic theory to the interpretation of events demands a much more formal training than study of a book like this can give, as well as a great deal of practice. One has, however, to start somewhere, and the following pages are offered to students and the general reader in the hope that they will enable, and encourage them to make a start.

The chief sources to which I am indebted will be evident to any economists who may look at this book. I should mention particularly, however, the work of Mr Colin Clark to which all who deal with international comparisons of economic magnitudes owe so much, the great volume of material which emerges from the United Nations and its specialized agencies, and from the Organization for European Economic Co-operation, and Professor Arthur Lewis's great survey of the causes of economic growth.

CONTENTS

CONTENTS

CHAPTER 1

Economies and their Outcomes

What an Economy is

AN economy, in the sense in which the word will mostly be used in this book, is a system by which people get a living. The British economy, for instance, is the whole collection of farms, factories, mines, shops, banks, ships, roads, railways, aircraft, offices, schools, cinemas, hospitals, houses, and the rest—looked at not as features in the landscape, but as going concerns, fully manned—which provide the British people with the goods and services which they either use themselves or sell abroad in order to be able to buy imports. We can describe in corresponding ways the American economy, the whole world economy, or, at the other end of the scale, the economy of the City of Leeds or of the parish of Far Headingley.

The simplest kind of economy is one in which one person has to provide all the goods and services he uses, and has nothing to do with anyone else. Robinson Crusoe has for a long time provided economics textbooks with their favourite example of this, but the essence of most economies is a very high degree of specialization by the various producers in them, and, in consequence, enormous complexity. The number of different occupations which people attribute to themselves in British censuses runs to about 30,000 and even for its own purposes of classification the census needs about 700 different occupational headings. The number of different products is also enormous—British exports are classified under some 2,500 headings, many of which, in turn, cover a considerable variety of different goods.

All this means that any economy, except the very simplest kind, is a system of parts which depend upon each other in an extremely complicated way. A factory worker, for instance, may be one of thousands who are directly engaged as a team in his factory (and perhaps in other factories concerned with earlier and later processes) on the production of a particular line of goods (say glass bottles or nylon socks) which may be used by hundreds of thousands or even millions of people. If we take into account the indirect membership of the productive team—the people who manufacture the machinery it uses, or the machinery that helps to make that machinery—the

11

scope of the interrelations involved in the production and sale of even one kind of good may expand to include portions of nearly every kind of productive organization in the economy. Moreover, the people who ultimately use the bottles or socks in question will be able to do so only because they earn money by taking part in 'teams' of equal complexity producing other goods. The demand for any particular kind of good depends upon the simultaneous, or slightly previous, production of all the other kinds.

The system of interrelations between the parts of an economy is thus so complicated that the task of studying it becomes rather like that of studying the physiology of a plant or an animal—which, like an economy, is made up of a vast number of units (cells in the one case, families in the other) each specialized to do one of a great many different jobs, and depending for its welfare on the working of the whole system. An economy is, indeed, in one sense harder to study than an animal or a plant, because it is not practicable to try experiments with it—the student has to be content with watching what he can see of its working in whatever combination and sequence of external circumstances the course of history may send. The questions which an economist asks about an economy are, nevertheless, rather similar to those which a biologist asks about his subject matter, and this analogy may help us to appreciate some, though by no means all, of the aspects of economies in general, and of the world economy as a whole, with which this book is concerned.

On Studying an Economy

Perhaps the first question to ask concerns the nature of what we may call the essential vital process of an economy. With living things these processes include feeding, digestion, and growth; with economies they include production, consumption, investment, and (again) growth. Any scientific study is concerned, wherever possible, with measurement, and we shall see that the measurement and comparison (between different economies, or for one economy between different times) of the rate at which these processes go on is a central one for economists.

Perhaps the second question which it is natural to ask about an economy is one with which the analogy from biology is less obvious. It concerns the way in which it is organized to carry out the vital processes which have just been mentioned. Does some central authority decide what shall be produced, and who shall produce it, and who shall get the products, or are these things determined, like the course of a highly improvised game of football, by the efforts of a large number of people towards different immediate objectives of

their own, without any central organization? While the vital processes are essentially of the same nature in all economies, the degree
in which they are governed by central organization, the nature of
that organization (where it exists), and the nature of the game which
is played between the various families and organizations in the
economy in the absence of central direction are matters which differ
widely from one economy to another.

We shall see, however, that in large economies, central control by
an authority is not normally anything like complete and has sometimes not existed at all, and this brings us to a point at which the
analogy between the study of an economy and that of an animal
becomes closer again. Where, as normally happens, people have
specialized jobs, so that they do not produce all of the things they
and their families need, and are at the same time not simply issued
by the authorities with what they are to have of the economy's
output of goods and services, a central feature of the economy must
be a monetary system. Each person taking part in production must
either be paid with, or must be able to exchange his product for,
something which he can use as general purchasing-power which, in
turn, he can use to buy the things he wants. The circulation of this
purchasing-power in any economy (except the rare ones which are
entirely centrally directed) is rather like the circulation of the blood
in an animal. The rate at which it goes on varies with, and can be
used with due care as a measure of, the level of vital activity in the
system as a whole, and in some degree affects the activity of all or
most of its specialized parts.

The fact that a change in the activity of any part of an economy
affects other parts through the monetary mechanism, and that
changes in those parts in turn affect the others (including the part
where the initial change took place) has some very interesting
consequences. It means that certain changes (particularly increases
or decreases in activity), once started, tend to reinforce themselves,
up to a point, at least. The level of activity in the economy as a
whole shows a reluctance to remain steady which gives those
responsible for economic policy some of their worst headaches. In
this, economies are considerably more troublesome to those concerned with their welfare than are animals or plants, which have
great capacities for adjusting themselves to changes in their
circumstances without unnecessary fuss.

Growth is the other great function which economies display in
common with living things, but here, as elsewhere, the analogy must
not be pressed too far. Economies grow, it is true, by diverting part
of their resources from being currently used up and directing them

into the equivalent of 'body-building'. To some extent, also, growth in an economy consists simply in its getting bigger—increasing the scale of its use of all kinds of resources and its output of all kinds of products. More significantly, however, it often involves the increase of output more than in proportion to any increase which there may be in the number of people in it or the amount of work they do—an increase in their output per head and their standard of living. This is made possible by changes in the methods of production—a change in the detail and efficiency (as distinct from the broad nature) of the vital processes of the economy to which living things show no very obvious counterpart. These changes, moreover, involve changes in the structure of the economy, by which we mean changes in the proportions of the people in it who do each kind of job, and also the creation of new kinds of job and the total disappearance of some old ones. Animals and plants in the course of growth also change their shapes, but with economies, it is the change in the standard of living they have reached rather than change in total size (as measured by their output) that tends to be associated with change in their structure. In a poor economy which is self-sufficient, for instance, over 70 per cent of the population may be farmers or their families; in a rich economy (also self-sufficient) the corresponding proportion may be only 10 or 15 per cent.

What Economies Provide

It is thus a feature of economies that their structures change and that this change puts the jobs of particular people in jeopardy. We have seen, too, that the level of activity in an economy is hard to keep steady (or to keep on a steadily rising path), so that there is a good deal of insecurity even apart from changes in structure. The most important questions about an economy, however, are perhaps those concerned, not with this uncertainty of its provision for the people in it, or even with its rate of growth, but with the general level of productiveness it has achieved, in relation to the number of people it has to support. It is in this that the economies of nations, and of regions of the world, differ perhaps most strikingly from one another.

These differences between the average provision which different economies make for the people in them are, in the nature of things, difficult to measure, but it is important to try since where a community's material standard of living stands in the wide range of variation which is to be seen in the world is a matter which affects every phase of its life. Let us start, therefore, with some of the obvious and measurable differences, and try to generalize later.

First, what is the range of difference in the adequacy with which different economies feed their people? If we measure average food consumption per head in one of the most usual ways, by the energy-providing power of the diet, expressed in Calories—the range is surprisingly small; the values recorded for India, China, or the West Indies may be only 20 or 30 per cent. less than those for the United States or the United Kingdom. But qualitatively there is a very great difference. Diets in poor countries consist overwhelmingly of vegetable foods, often of a monotonous and sometimes unappetizing kind—rice in Asia, maize porridge in much of Africa and eastern Europe. They contain little fat or meat, and are some-times deficient in constituents necessary to health. On the other hand, the diets of rich populations are largely derived from animals, either as meat or as dairy produce, and are altogether more varied.

In clothing, the contrast between the consumption of rich and poor communities is more obvious. The wealthy countries of western Europe and North America use from three to eight times as much of the main clothing fibres per head of their populations as India or China do. To some extent, of course, this is a matter of climate, but by no means entirely—parts of China have a climate as severe as any thickly inhabited region of the world. The variation in clothing consumption depends much more on means than needs. The same is true of housing. Information about this is very incomplete, but we know that, for instance, while in the United States or the United Kingdom more than four-fifths of the houses have more than one room to each person living in them, and about the same propor-tion have running water laid on, the great majority of houses in oriental countries, the Middle East, the Caribbean region, much of eastern Europe and the U.S.S.R. have more than two people to a room, and only a minority have running water. Without making any allowance for differences in facilities, it may be said that in the poorer countries there is only a fifth or a tenth as much houseroom in relation to population as there is in the richest.

But what is still more striking is that, while the poorest com-munities spend 80 or 90 per cent. of their incomes on food, clothing and housing, the richest communities not only have much more of these essentials but have more than half their incomes left for other things after they have paid for them. Broadly speaking, the rich countries manage to get about three times as much of the services of teachers and about ten times as much medical and hospital service in relation to their populations as the poor ones, but the really big discrepancies—differences of a hundredfold or more—lie in such matters as the number of radios or motor cars or the consumption of newsprint per thousand of the population.

The Difficulties of Comparison

It is these great differences between the relative amounts of different goods or services which two communities may be found to have per thousand of their populations which make it difficult to generalize further—to say that one of the two communities is, for instance, twice as well off as the other. In some kinds of goods it may be no better off, in others twenty times as well off; how are we to make a general comparison? This difficulty is one which economists encounter frequently, just because, as we have noted, their business is, largely, to try to sum up, in quantitative terms as far as possible, the main facts about economies; and economies are so complex that complete and detailed statements about them would be hopelessly clumsy. The obvious way out of it in the case in question —where we are trying to make a summary comparison of the amounts of all goods and services per head in two different economies—is to use some kind of average of the ratios between the amount of a good per head in one country and the amount of the same good per head in the other. But what kind of average? Should the ratio of consumptions of matches count as much in the average as that of the consumptions of bread?

Clearly it should not; the ratios of the amounts consumed per head of the various kinds of goods should be 'weighted' in some way so as to reflect the differing importances of these goods. But this brings us to the real difficulty. The relative importance of the different kinds of good may, as we have seen, be quite different in different countries. Motor cars and their running are of great importance in the United States, where expenditure on them is over a third of that on food; in the west European countries their importance is much less, expenditure on them being only something between a fifteenth and a fortieth of expenditure on food. In comparing total consumption per head in the United States with that in Europe, should we give food and motor cars the relative importance which they have in the American way of life or the European? Which we do may clearly make a good deal of difference to the answer we get.

This is the difficulty known as the 'index number problem'; it is in principle insoluble, since one country's consumption-pattern is just as good a basis for comparison as the other's. In practice, a compromise or average is made between the two patterns in order to get a set of 'weights' reflecting the relative importance, for the purpose of the comparison, of different kinds of goods and services. But the compromise is bound to be an arbitrary one, and the more the consumption-patterns of the two countries in question differ, the greater is the inevitable margin of uncertainty attached to any comparison between their average consumptions per head, or standards of living. The average consumption and use per head of all goods and services in the United States was, in 1950, 3·3 times as great as that in Italy if American expenditures are taken as representing the relative importance of different things, but 5·6 times as great if Italian expenditures are taken for this purpose. In comparing the United States with India in this way the margin of uncertainty would be much greater.

There are other difficulties in making such comparisons. One is that we have not usually got information about all the goods and services which are used or rendered in a country. The services of housewives in looking after children, cleaning, and cooking, for instance, are not recorded, and are generally not estimated, though they obviously play an important part in making the standard of living what it is—a part, moreover, which is probably much more important, in relation to the total consumption of goods and services, in poor countries than in rich ones.

Nevertheless, so long as the difficulties and ambiguities of quantitative comparisons between the livings which different economies afford to their inhabitants are kept in mind, such numerical comparisons are well worth making. Perhaps the best way of making them for our present purpose is to look at the relations between successive pairs of economies which are not too far apart in the scale. Take, first, the United States and the United Kingdom. The former stood, in 1950, some 60 or 100 per cent. (according to the basis of comparison) above the latter. It is worth noting, however, that there are very considerable regional differences within the United States, the contrast between the rich areas of the middle Atlantic seaboard and the far west and the poor area of the south east being probably just about as great as that between the United States average, and the United Kingdom. In the richest parts of the United States, a total population of nearly fifty million lives at an average level which is more than twice the British on any basis of reckoning. ·

The other countries of north-western Europe do not differ very much from the United Kingdom in their standard of living; the general tendency is for them to be a little below. When we come to Italy, however, we find a contrast with the United Kingdom which in 1950 was perhaps rather similar to that between the latter and

B

the richest parts of the United States—the average amount of goods and services per head was between two and three times as great in the United Kingdom as in Italy, though the contrast has probably diminished somewhat in the intervening years. Among the countries where the average amount of goods and services per head is not very different from that in Italy are the Soviet Union and (a little lower) Japan.

If we go down to about half the Italian level, we come to, or perhaps rather below, the living standards of the poorest countries in Europe (if we exclude Turkey)—Greece, Yugoslavia, and Albania—and into a group which includes most of the Caribbean countries and the poorer countries of South America. But these still stand to India much as California or New York stands to the United Kingdom, or the United Kingdom to Italy. And India is by no means at the bottom of the scale; China perhaps stands to her roughly as the United Kingdom stands to the United States, and there are very considerable populations in tropical Africa and elsewhere whose provision is smaller still.

It seems from this that the average provisions which considerable economies make for their people are spread over a range which, according to the method of measurement, can be computed as anything from rather less than twentyfold to over a hundredfold—the ratios for communities so diverse as the richest and the poorest in the world have little meaning, except that the contrast is very great. The reader may well ask what this contrast means in terms of welfare or happiness. The answer, unfortunately, can only be a vague one. We can say, for instance, that the expectation of life for a newly-born child is less than half as long in the poorest countries for which we have the information as in the richest, and that the incidence of malnutrition and of diseases which keep people chronically at less than full vigour is much higher in poor countries. These differences, on the other hand, while in part inevitable concomitants of the differences in the general standard of living, are by no means wholly so; to a large extent poor health is a result not so much of poverty itself as of the ignorance and the bad or weak administration to which the poverty also is partly due. It is possible for a community to be at least fairly healthy without being rich.

As for happiness, there is no way of measuring it. There is, however, some presumption that an economy which gives people a wide scope for choosing the kinds of work and leisure which suit them, and which preserves them from extreme poverty or the threat of economic disaster, will be more satisfactory than one which does not. A very poor economy cannot do these things; it can offer only the prospect of:

> Cold, pain and labour and all human ills,
> And mighty poets in their misery dead,

which Wordsworth, not unnaturally, found so unpleasing. And, for the world as a whole, it is still poverty which is the issue. The average provision of goods and services which the world economy makes for its inhabitants is perhaps roughly equivalent to that which, in British social surveys, defines the 'poverty line'—the minimum material standard of living judged necessary in British conditions to maintain full health and efficiency, below which some 2 or 3 per cent. of the British population now lives.

At all events, for the purposes of this book it may be sufficient to regard an economy as a system for providing people with their livings, and to enquire how adequately and by what mechanism it does it, both in particular national economies and in the world economy as a whole, without asking too many questions about human satisfaction with the outcome. To this more mundane task we must now turn.

CHAPTER 2

The Essentials of an Economy

The Vital Processes—Production, Consumption, and Investment
AN economy being, essentially, a system by which people get a living, there are two principal kinds of process which must go on in it more or less continuously. The first is what is generally called production. The instances of it that come first to mind are perhaps such things as the growing of food on farms or the making in factories of the goods that will satisfy people's wants—clothes, medicines, television receivers, or whatever it may be. But economists have long been driven to take a much wider view of production than might be suggested by instances like these. If the assembly of a television receiver in the factory is production, what about the display and selling of it in a shop, without which it would not (or would not so conveniently) get to a user? Or what about the servicing of it when it goes wrong? Or what, again, about the work of the engineers and performers who provide the programmes for it to receive? All these, and many other services are, clearly, necessary if the 'living' which some people in the economy get is to include the possibility of watching television, and they are accordingly regarded as part of the economy's production. Indeed, it will do if we say that production includes any activity, and the provision of any service, which satisfies, or is expected to satisfy a want. Having defined production so widely, we must hasten to add that, when it comes to counting and measuring, there are certain parts of production, in the widest sense, which economists are obliged to ignore because they have not enough information about them—the enormous quantity of work done by housewives in their homes, as we have seen, receives this rather unchivalrous treatment.

The second group of processes essential to an economy is, of course, consumption—the receipt of services and the use of material goods to satisfy wants. It must be thought of in the same inclusive way as production—not limited to the using up of material goods—and, on the other hand, if there are any goods or services which, for practical reasons, we exclude from the catalogue of production (as we normally exclude the services of housewives in the home), then we must exclude the enjoyment of these things or services from the

20

catalogue of consumption as well. There are, moreover, some further practical points which arise when one tries actually to catalogue the consumption which goes on in an economy. Strictly speaking, consumption is the act of satisfying one's wants. A pair of trousers satisfies (in part) the wearer's wants for warmth and for a decorous and fashionable appearance as long as he is wearing them, and, even when he is not, the possession of them contributes to his sense of security. The 'consumption' of the trousers, therefore, may be said to go on as long as they are in the possession of anyone who is wearing, or might wear them. Much the same can be said about any goods which render their services over a considerable length of time—particularly the long-lived ones like furniture. In general however, economists and statisticians have inadequate information about the quantities of such goods that are in the households of the economy, or about the lengths of time over which they continue to render services—to be 'consumed'. On the other hand, they usually have more adequate information about the acquisition of these goods by households; they therefore take this as the criterion of consumption. Not only food, but clothing, furniture, and even motor cars are recorded as being 'consumed' in the year, the quarter or the month (whichever we are studying) in which a household first acquires them. The only long-lived things actually in the possession of their users which are recorded as rendering their services year by year over the whole of their useful physical lives are dwelling-houses.

So far as personal service like those of doctors, waiters, or bus-drivers are concerned, the production of the service and the consumption or receipt of it take place at the same time. With material goods, however, it is different. Not only do such goods emerge in their finished form only after undergoing a number of manufacturing processes (perhaps preceded by mining or growing of the materials and fuels used on the way), but they take time to pass from one process to the other and, after they are in their finished physical condition, still more time to pass through warehouses and shops into the possession of consumers. For every kind of finished good, in fact, there is a sort of 'pipeline', or rather a system of pipelines, stretching from the original sources of the materials used to the consumer. Unless these pipelines have something in them at every part of the way, production at the next stage will be held up. These stocks or 'inventories' of materials, goods in process or waiting for the next process, and finished goods in course of distribution may either increase or decrease in any year. If they increase it is because production is going on faster than consumption; if consumption is going on faster than production, they decrease. The accumulation of stocks through an excess of production of goods over consumption of them is a part of the process described as 'investment'—more precisely it is the part of it often called 'inventory investment'. It can, as we have just noted, be either negative or positive, in that stocks can be run down as well as built up. If it is negative—if stocks are running down—the process is often called 'disinvestment'.

There is, however, another and quantitatively more important respect in which what is produced can (and usually does) differ from what is consumed in an economy. There are many products which are not designed to satisfy the wants of consumers directly at all; industrial machinery, factory buildings, cargo ships, lorries, and, indeed, all means of transport in so far as they are intended to carry goods rather than people. Moreover, since houses are regarded (rightly) as providers of services which are 'consumed' over the many years of their life, the building of a house is not to be thought of as satisfying a want (except to a very small extent) in the year in which it was built; it is, like the building of a clothing factory or the sinking of a mine-shaft, a piece of production for the future. Such production for the future is called 'fixed investment'; the things thus stored up by the community are 'fixed capital'. But while items added to fixed capital are not consumed quickly or soon, they are, of course, consumed eventually. If nothing is done to keep them in repair, they wear out; even if they are properly maintained, there comes, in many cases, a time when it is better to replace them with new items than to repair them any more. A good deal of the production of an economy, therefore, is concerned with 'maintenance and depreciation'—that is to say, with keeping fixed capital in repair and replacing it as it wears out.

This gives us a useful classification of the activities which go on in an economy. Their outcomes can perhaps best be visualized as streams or flows of goods and services. Ultimately, the economist is interested in making suitable measurements of these flows, but for the time being it may be best to postpone this and to visualize the flows as concretely as possible as heterogeneous streams of goods and services. First there is the stream of goods and services produced; the product of the economy, which is also called its income. (For some purposes it is convenient to exclude from consideration those products which are destined for maintenance and depreciation of capital, in which case we speak of 'net income' or 'net product'; otherwise the income or product is described as 'gross'.) Part of the product, as we have seen, flows through the 'pipeline' of inventories to the consumers—who may take out of it either more or less than is being put in—and part goes to add to (and, if we are reckoning income 'gross', another part to maintain and replace) the stock of fixed capital.

Wealth, Factors of Production, and Growth
But to get a first comprehensive view of an economy these flows of goods and services must be seen in relation to the stocks of resources at the disposal of the economy, which enable production to take place and which constitute its wealth. Wealth may be defined as 'anything which is useful, directly or indirectly, for satisfying wants'. This may sound at first rather like a definition of the product or income of the economy, which we have just been considering; but they are really quite different. Income, as we have noted, is the rate of flow of the stream of goods and services. Wealth is the stock of useful things or qualities—all the useful things and qualities in the economy which could be revealed by an instantaneous photograph of it (supposing that qualities could be photographed), and just as an instantaneous photograph of a stream can never, directly, show it as flowing, so the flow of income is not the same as a catalogue of wealth—though the two things are related to each other.

What kinds of thing and quality are included in wealth? First, perhaps, since we have mentioned it already, we may put fixed capital, the stocks of machines, factories, transport equipment, dwellings, and other apparatus for producing goods and services which have been accumulated by the activity of the economy in the past. Secondly, also mentioned already, there are the 'inventories'—stocks of raw materials and foodstuffs, semi-manufactured goods, and finished products which we have thought of as filling the 'pipe-line' between different stages of production, or between the last stage of production and the consumer. (Strictly also, we should include the stocks of all kinds of useful things which have come into the possession of households and have not yet exhausted their capacity to render services.)

Next, perhaps, we may have natural resources of all kinds—land and climate of kinds favourable to growing crops, minerals, navigable waters, sources of water power, and the rest. It is not easy in practice to draw a satisfactory line between these natural resources and 'capital'. Agricultural land, for instance, as we know it, is largely the product of improvement by man—nearly all of Great Britain was under forest two thousand years ago, and so was the United States westward to the Mississippi only two hundred years ago. The distinction between 'capital' which is in some degree man-made, and natural resources, which in principle are not, does not, however, matter; an arbitrary division between them will do quite well.

Finally we come to human beings, with all their qualities and abilities. To include them in a catalogue of wealth may convey to some a suggestion of a slave system and to others a flavour of sentimentality, but neither interpretation is justified; the logic of the situation is clear. If wealth is the stock of things and qualities useful in satisfying wants, then a large part of it is human. The fact that the people in an economy are also the agents in relation to whose satisfaction the usefulness of wealth is assessed is equally important, but quite distinct.

The human qualities in question are enormously varied. They include the sheer physical ability to do work, but also willingness to do it for the rewards that it enables to be offered; the ability of some to organize production, but also the will; the social qualities that enable people to get on together in productive enterprises, but also the qualities that enable them to form reasonably stable and orderly political communities. Perhaps above all, the human component of wealth includes technical knowledge. Although all the main forms of wealth which we have mentioned are necessary to make an economy productive, it may be argued that knowledge of how to set about producing is a peculiarly basic requirement—that an economy which is poor in natural resources and (to begin with) in capital also can generally build up an outfit of capital and prosper in spite of its meagre natural endowment of land and minerals if only it knows enough. Perhaps the only quality which might be claimed to be more basic than knowledge is the will to get a good living—on the ground that where there's a will a way is likely soon to be found. But, in fact, the will to acquire and use more knowledge for getting a better living seems often to be stimulated by nothing so much as the demonstration—or the discovery—of what technical knowledge can do; the knowledge and the will grow together. It might certainly be claimed with some force that this knowledge (and the accompanying will to use it) have been among the strongest influences favouring those particular forms of government and those particular social institutions which, in turn, make for technical progress.

But this discussion of the qualities which are included in an economy's wealth is taking us too far afield. The immediate point to be noted is that the uses or services of the various different kinds of wealth, which are required for productive processes, are what economists generally call the 'factors of production'—the services of people (with all their skills, abilities, and knowledge), the services of goods already produced (including both fixed capital and stocks in store or undergoing some process), and the services of natural resources and amenities. All of these, or some of their sub-species, are in use at any given time in co-operation with each other for the production of every kind of good and most kinds of service that compose the economy's output, for services usually require some equipment and materials as well as human skill and exertion. Wealth, in short, provides factors of production, which in combination with each other generate the economy's income. The greater part of that income is consumed, giving the community whatever standard of living it enjoys, but the rest is 'fed back' (to use an engineering term) as investment in order to maintain and perhaps to increase the stock of capital which is a part of the economy's wealth. This connection between the rate of investment and the rate of growth of a part of wealth, from which, with the other parts, production flows, implies that investment is connected with the rate at which the income of the economy is able to increase.

The ways in which income influences the growth of wealth, and therefore the future growth of income, are not, however confined to this. The part of income which is consumed also has something to do with the maintenance and increase of wealth, and so of income. Food, clothing, entertainment, medical attention, education, the services of houses, and the other items that the consumer receives affect not only his health and sense of well-being, but also his ability and willingness to help in production. They also affect the number of children who survive and (in less obvious ways) the number born, and thus the rate of increase of the working population. The size and composition of consumption are, of course, by no means the only influences affecting these things, and the strength, and even the direction, of the effect which a change in them will have on the size and rate of growth of the human part of wealth is sometimes far from clear. But the point is that they either do, or may be presumed to affect it, sometimes very drastically. Even when we reduce the working of an economy to its most essential elements, the interrelations which we see are by no means simple, and many of them lie outside the field in which economists normally work. To some of the predominantly economic relations between consumption, investment, and the expansion of the economy we shall, however, have to return in Chapter 7.

How is it Organized?
The account which has just been given applies to any economy at all, whether it is capitalist or communist, primitive or highly

developed. But we have said nothing so far about the ways in which production, investment, or the distribution of the product to the consumer are organized or regulated. These, of course, are matters in which one economy differs widely from another.

The simplest sort of economy to understand, at first sight—apart from Robinson Crusoe on his island—is one in which these essential activities of the economy are planned and enforced by some kind of central authority, which determines what everyone concerned shall produce (or try to produce), what they shall receive for consumption, what, in consequence, shall be left over for investment, and how it shall be applied. The clearest examples of such an economy are, perhaps, to be found in monastic communities, or military states like ancient Sparta, but on a smaller scale we have the peasant family living entirely on its own produce, in which what is to be done is determined by the head or heads of the family, or perhaps by some kind of family council, often very much guided by tradition. Sometimes the 'family' in which things are ordered in this way is quite a large one, amounting to a whole clan or village; sometimes it is small. The essential point is that production is planned and the products are allocated. There are still quite a lot of large economies consisting mainly of such self-sufficient groups; they are usually referred to, rather misleadingly, as 'subsistence economies', because all, or nearly all that is produced is used for subsistence by the families that produce it. It was estimated, for instance, that in Kenya and French West Africa over 70 per cent. of the labour expended in 1950 went to produce goods which were not marketed. The importance of such economies, however, is steadily diminishing as transport improves and the incentives, and the opportunities, to earn money either by going out to work, or by selling produce, increase.

On a larger scale we have the modern military state, that is to say, the modern state as it is organized for total war. In the later part of the second world war, all the main belligerents, but especially the United Kingdom, the Soviet Union and Germany got fairly near to complete central organization of their economies. Everyone's occupation was fixed, and could be changed, by order; what firms were to produce was almost completely determined by order (at least in the sense that they got raw materials only for approved purposes), and though civilians continued to be paid wholly and the forces partly in money, what they could buy with it was so narrowly limited by rationing that nearly all of output was in effect being allocated either to war purposes or to ration-card holders for their personal use.

The difficulties of the centrally administered economy may seem at first sight to be difficulties of administration rather than economic difficulties in the ordinary sense. Apart from the sheer political problems of carrying decisions into effect, however, the authorities in such an economy are still faced by what is essentially an economic problem—one, indeed, which some people, rather confusingly, call 'the economic problem'—namely, how to use a limited amount of resources to the best effect, bearing in mind that they can be used both in different technical ways for the same purpose and also for different purposes, and that what is used for one purpose is not available for any of the others. Merely to understand that this problem exists is, indeed, the beginning of wisdom (though it is certainly very far from being the end of it) for economic planners, and those who are concerned with economic policy generally. The most general principle that applies to this disposal of resources is that they are being laid out to the best effect when they seem to be equally scarce in every use; that is to say, when a small amount of any resource, transferred from one use to any other, seems to give equally satisfactory results in any of them. In ordinary economic life, the next problem (with which we need not be concerned at the moment) is, of course, how to get any indication of the satis-factoriness of these results, from the point of view of the community as a whole. In war, this problem may be much easier; there is one overriding object—victory—and there may be some objective ground for judging whether a merchant ship, a heavy bomber, or a squadron of fighters (which may represent alternative uses of about the same amount of basic resources) will make the greatest contri-bution to it.

Apart from these general judgements on the best use of resources, however, there is always, in peace or war, a very great difficulty in planning the activity of an economy, because the technical relations between different kinds of output are so complicated. To build ships, for instance, requires not only the steel and other materials which go into the ship, but also steel-making and machine-building equip-ment, which in turn require more steel (along with other things) and, incidentally, more shipping capacity. The working out of the full implications of the decision to expand production in any direction, or of any programme of production for final use, is a vastly com-plicated matter which has been tackled really systematically only in recent years.

Nevertheless, although central planning of output is difficult (or, at least, difficult to do well), the objections to it are not usually so strong as those to central planning of distribution, in the sense of deciding exactly what consumers' goods each family is to have, and issuing them to it. In a war emergency, when there is no room for the production of anything but necessities, and it is of the utmost importance that these necessities should be distributed in accordance with the physiological need for them it may be the best, or the only way, but otherwise it encounters difficulties from the mere fact that tastes differ. It was to adapt what was otherwise a rigid system of rationing to this fact that in the United Kingdom 'points rationing' was introduced in the second world war—the 'points' issued in ration books were essentially a form of money which could be used to buy any of a variety of foodstuffs. (Ordinary money was, of course, required for the purchases as well, but it was generally the supply of 'points' that limited them.) In fact, it is mainly because what a person, or a family, will most want differs so much from one case to another, and, indeed, with the same person or family from one week to another, that there is such great convenience in distributing the products of the economy, not by direct allocation, but through markets, in exchange for money. It is not surprising that this is almost universally done in normal times except in so far as families live on their own produce.

One of the most important types of economy in the modern world (the Soviet Union being the leading example) is that in which production is centrally planned, but consumers' goods are distributed through the market. Let us consider how this works. Nearly all production in the Soviet Union is governed by a plan for a five-year period, with firmer plans for each year as it comes. These plans embody the main political decisions about the division of resources between consumption, investment and armaments. They are worked out in great detail, as to different types of goods to be produced, are submitted to the individual industrial plants and farms for discussion, and are modified in the light of what is thus learnt about their feasibility. Of the goods and services produced, those destined for investment, military, or social purposes are, of course, allocated in accordance with the plan (they are also paid for, though that is not what determines where they shall go). Consumers' goods, however, are sold in the market—their ultimate destination depending, in this case, on who chooses to buy them.

The prices of goods thus sold to consumers consist mainly of their costs of production and handling plus a purchase-tax, frequently large, which is the principal instrument by which the authorities can regulate the prices charged in the shops. Presumably their aim is so to regulate the price of each kind of good that the amount which people will want to buy will be about equal to the amount actually available. If the price is too high, there will be a piling up of unsold goods, which could be stopped (and which one would expect the authorities to want to stop promptly) by lowering the price. If, on the other hand, price is too low, the good in question will be sold out some time before the next batch is delivered to the shops; in extreme cases there may be queues to buy it, the people at the back of the queue being disappointed. A moderate error in this direction by the planning authorities does not matter much except with regard to the basic foodstuffs, and it seems that some goods, such as television receivers, have in some years been quite heavily under-priced in this sense of the term.

Even in an economy where production is rigidly planned, however, it is not always thought necessary for the authorities to regulate the prices of consumers' goods at all. In principle, it is perfectly possible for whatever is produced for consumers to be put on sale and allowed to find its own price. If, for instance, the sellers pursue a policy of getting rid of each month's batch of goods (or perhaps each week's or each day's) before the next batch comes from the factories, then, if towards the end of the period they still have a good deal on hand, they will lower the price just as much as they find necessary to clear their stocks. On the other hand, if sellers are running short some time before new supplies are expected, the buyers who want to buy before then will tend to bid against each other for what is left, so that the less keen, or those who can afford less, will be induced by the raised prices to wait. With a free market, therefore (that is to say, one in which prices are free to move), there is some presumption that prices will vary so that stocks neither pile up nor become completely exhausted. Free markets do not in fact always work satisfactorily in this respect, but they often do, and they have played not unimportant parts even in otherwise closely controlled economies. In a number of east European countries during and after the war for instance, while rations were sold at fixed prices, goods over the ration, or unrationed goods, were bought and sold legally in free markets. Russian collective farms, also, have been allowed to sell in free local markets the excess of their produce over what they have contracted to deliver at fixed prices to the state.

Whenever the products are sold for money, whether at prices fixed by the authorities or at prices which are allowed to find their own level, the state of demand for those products will, at any rate, make itself known to the authorities, either through what happens to prices or through what happens to stocks in the shops. These market indications need not limit the authorities very seriously in their production planning. If (as in the Soviet Union) the amount which consumers have to spend is much greater than the cost of production of all the available consumers' goods[1], the whole of this difference can be gathered in either as purchase tax or as profits of the state enterprises producing or selling the goods in question. There is therefore a very wide range over which the state is free to increase its output of one kind of good and decrease that of another, thus lowering the price realizable for the first and raising that which can be got for the second, without actually reducing the price of any good below cost of production. Even if there were not this margin of spending-power over cost of production of consumers' goods, the state would still be under no necessity to produce goods in the precise quantities at which, at prices equal to cost of production, consumers would want to buy them, so long as it did not mind making a loss on some goods which could be set off against its profits on others.

The third main type of economy is that in which neither production nor distribution of goods and services is regulated in detail by any central authority, being governed by conditions in the markets. Here, again, it is hard to find a pure example of this type at present, though the United Kingdom's economy came near to it two generations ago, and that of the United States only one generation ago, and both of these economies, and most others west of the Iron Curtain are still essentially closer to this pattern than to any other that can be simply described. The essence of such an economy is that goods and services are produced to be sold for money, by organizations which are interested in making profits, and which cannot carry on indefinitely if they do not. In such an economy, what is produced in the way of consumers' goods, at least, is fairly closely governed by the way in which consumers choose to lay out their incomes. Prices of goods may be either fixed by their producers in some sort of relation to cost of production, or allowed to find their own level in a free market. In the former case there will be unsatisfied demand for some goods and unsaleable stocks of others will accumulate, unless production stands in a close relation to what people are willing to buy at the prices fixed. If prices are allowed to find their own level, on the other hand, producers of some goods will make larger profits than those of others (some may make losses) unless the output levels of different goods are, again, in a particular

---

[1] This is because consumers get their incomes not only by making consumers' goods, but by making armaments and capital goods as well, and very little of their incomes, thus earned, are removed from them by direct taxation.

relation to the relative demands for them. Under either system of pricing, there is some pressure towards adjustment; firms which cannot sell their output must reduce it or perhaps go out of business; firms which could sell more than they are producing have an inducement, and probably an opportunity, to expand production, as have new firms to set up in lines of production that are doing well. Similarly firms making losses must eventually change their ways or go out of business, while those making small profits have less inducement and probably less opportunity to expand, and are less likely to be joined by new competitors in the same line of business, than those which are making big profits. Expansion tends to happen where demand is big relatively to production, no expansion, or actual contraction, where it is the other way about. The unregulated economy is subject to a number of serious ills, and does not always work smoothly, but the fact that production is not centrally regulated in detail does not mean that it has no tendency to conform to any particular pattern.

This third kind of economy, in which production is regulated mainly by the force of the market, is not to be necessarily identified with private enterprise. It is true that a private enterprise economy— one in which the state does not produce goods and services for sale, and in which any private person or organization is free to do so—will necessarily be of this type, but the converse is not necessarily true. While state enterprises are perhaps more likely to receive subsidy, or for other reasons to be independent of the pressures of the market, than is the case with private organizations, their independence of it is generally partial and may not exist at all. A number of the nationalized industries in the United Kingdom are under statutory obligation to cover their costs, at any rate in the long run, which means that their output is intended, in the long run, to be market-controlled. Similarly, while freedom to enter a branch of production is part of the general notion of a private enterprise economy, and while such an economy is always market-regulated, it does not follow that freedom of entry is essential to market-regulated economies as such. Freedom of entry may not, in fact exist, either because there is a state monopoly (as with coal-mining in the United Kingdom) or because a great deal of capital is needed, and existing organizations are firmly entrenched (as with aluminium production in North America). Nevertheless, production is influenced by demand. Market conditions exert pressure on established firms, even monopolies, to expand one line of production or to contract another. For the purpose of deciding how, in the broadest sense, an economy works, the question whether production is governed by market conditions is more important than questions about the ownership of firms, freedom of entry into particular lines of production, or the kind of competition between firms which engage in it.

The broad distinctions between differently worked economies can therefore be summarized as follows: In the first place, there is the 'subsistence economy' which is really a collection of totally planned economies on a family or tribal scale, with no exchange of goods or services either between them or with the outside world. Next, there is the totally planned economy on a national scale, which is most nearly exemplified by the economies of the great powers in the second world war. In this, there is a high degree of specialization, but no exchange in the ordinary sense; people and organizations produce what they are told to produce and are given their rations. The monetary and pricing systems which in fact continued to exist in the war economies were, of course, tokens of the fact that a fully planned economy was not really attained, but they were deprived of a great part of their normal functions.

The other kinds of economy are in some degree exchange or market economies; to survive on any considerable scale they require a monetary system of some kind. They are of two main kinds; the production-planned economy and the wholly market-directed economy. In the former (e.g. the Soviet Union), productive organizations are told what to produce, but are paid in money, and their employees, also paid in money, are allowed to buy freely in the market. In the latter, there are no central directions about production, productive organizations seeking (or, at any rate, needing) to make profits, and having their activities therefore directed by conditions in the markets for goods and services. The next stage of the discussion will be limited to market economies in the broad sense—for the sufficient reason that they are of vastly greater importance than 'subsistence' or wholly planned economies in ordinary times. We shall have, however, to distinguish from time to time between those economies where everything, or nearly everything, depends on the market, and chose where production is mainly governed by central planning.

CHAPTER 3

The Flows of Money

MOST economies, as we have seen, are market economies in which individual families or productive enterprises do not produce most of what they themselves consume or store up, and do not themselves consume or store up most of what they produce—they sell most of their products for money and buy with money most of what they consume, or of what they add to their stocks of goods and equipment. In such an economy, therefore, most production is not simply an immediate attempt to meet the producers' wants, and, except where production is centrally planned, the aggregate investment which comes about is not the result merely of decisions that so much ought to be accumulated. Between production on the one hand and consumption or accumulation on the other there intervene one or more exchanges of goods or services against money.

The Circular Flow
In order to form a clear picture of the monetary machinery by which a market economy works, let us start with the simplest kind of situation, in which all output is produced by enterprises (not necessarily private) for sale, and in which there is no saving, no foreign trade, and no taxation. In such a community, a sum of money equal to the full value of output is paid out in each period by enterprises to the people who provide them with labour, capital, or materials, or who draw profits from them—that is to say, this sum is paid out to households. The whole of this money is then paid back by households to enterprises in exchange for the goods which they want to consume.

Now, it can be seen that, if the volume of production does not change, a simple system of this kind can go on working indefinitely, with a constant amount of money. Ignore profits for a moment and suppose that all the payments connected with production consist of wages, salaries, and similar items which are paid out at the end of each week. Then what households have in hand at the beginning of this week will be precisely the cost of producing last week's output, and by expending this sum during the week they can buy all of last week's output at a price equal to its cost of

33

production. Profits introduce a slight complication. In practice, of course, enterprises normally rely upon selling their output at a price which covers more than their out-of-pocket payments in connection with its production. If, however, we suppose that output is going on at the same level, week by week, the difficulty vanishes. It is true that there will not be enough money in households to buy last week's output at prices which allow for profits unless those profits have already been paid out, and that the profit on a particular batch of goods is not even earned until the goods are sold. With a constant output of goods week after week, however, there will always be some profits available in households to help buy the goods produced in the previous week, even though it is profit earned, not on those goods themselves, but on an earlier batch—perhaps the batch which was sold in the previous week and produced in the week before that. It is plain, then, that a steady stream of production, and its sale, can be financed by the circular flow of a fixed amount of money (how much is required we shall have to enquire later), between enterprises and households. If the volume of production is for any reason increased, there are further complications: the enterprises will have to find more money from somewhere to pay their increased wage-bill, etc., and households will also have to find some more in order to buy the first enlarged batch of goods on advance of receiving the enlarged profits on them; but that need not concern us at the moment.

It is more to the point to note that the assumption made above that there is no saving is very unrealistic. In any actual economy, both enterprises and households are liable to save; their savings may be regarded as passing straight into a 'capital market', from which it may be withdrawn again by either households or enterprises (in practice mostly the latter) which are prepared to borrow, normally in order principally to buy producers' durable goods. In fact, a good deal of the purchase of durable goods by enterprises is financed out of their own savings, without recourse to the capital market, but we may ignore this fact for the present, supposing that in this respect, as in regard to goods and services, the economy in question is in the highest degree an exchange economy, in which savings also all pass through a market. We may then modify the picture of the money flows in the economy into something like Diagram 1.

In this picture of the system, any excess of a household's or enterprise's income over its expenditure is regarded by definition as saving, and as flowing straight into the capital market. It is therefore in this market, and only there, that money can be thought

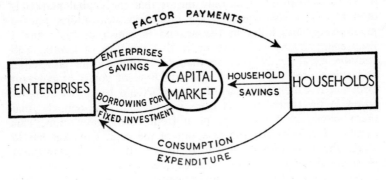

Diagram 1.

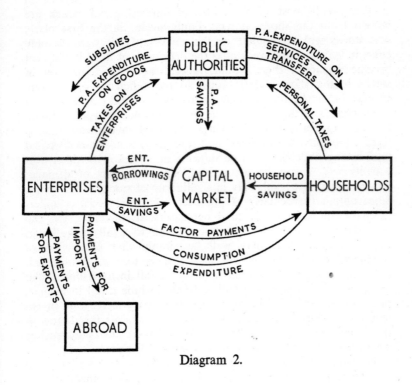

Diagram 2.

of as accumulating. (This only means that the capital market is thought of as embracing all the old socks, tea-caddies on the mantelpiece, and holes in the ground in which people actually keep spare money.) Now, in order that the flow of money shall continue at a steady level, so that it can finance the production and subsequent purchase of a steady flow of goods at constant prices, it is merely necessary that there should be no net accumulation in the capital market (thus comprehensively defined)—that there should be no leakage of it from active circulation. This means, of course, that the flow out of the capital market has to equal the flow into it, which is to say that fixed investment must equal the combined savings of households and enterprises.

What will happen if fixed investment falls short of this total? In this case, total expenditure on goods and services in the week in question will fall short of what is required to buy the previous week's output at the prices hitherto ruling for it. The effects of this will no doubt vary from one kind of good or service to another. With most of the kinds of finished goods which are bought from the shops, it will simply mean, in the first place, that stocks will accumulate on the shelves; if this were the only effect in (say) the first week after the deficiency of fixed investment became apparent, there would, indeed, be an accumulation of stocks in the shops exactly equal to the deficiency of demand. It may be noted that this accumulation of stocks is a kind of investment, and that in the case just mentioned it would exactly fill the gap between total savings and fixed investment—that is to say, total investment (fixed and inventory) would exactly equal total saving. Indeed, it can be shown that, somehow or other, this equality will always be maintained. The deficiency of demand, however, may not result only in a piling up of stocks in the shops. Some output (particularly of producers' durable goods) is undertaken to the order of the final purchasers. If, therefore, the gap between saving and fixed investment is due to a fall in the latter, the immediate effect may well be simply that production of producers' durable goods will fall—that is to say, income will fall. The further repercussions either of a fall in fixed investment or of an increase in saving will certainly include a fall in income, probably accompanied by an at least temporary increase in inventory investment—an increase which will be against the desires of the shopkeepers and merchants who find their stocks increasing. There may also be a reduction in some or all prices.

To pursue this piece of reasoning further would lead us into deep water; enough has perhaps been said to show that a steady rate of production and distribution of goods and services can be maintained with the help of the circulation of a fixed amount of money, but that if certain conditions fail to be fulfilled, the circulation of money, and with it, in some degree, the production and distribution of goods and services, will run down. Alternatively, if (in the system we have been discussing), fixed investment exceeds total saving and provided that more money can be drawn into active circulation, the circulation will expand, production probably expanding with it so long as there is no physical limit to its growth, and prices will probably rise.

Without pursuing any further for the present the conditions of a steady circulation of money and goods, or the consequences of a departure from them, it will now be useful to look a little more realistically at the form which the monetary circulation takes in actual economies. So far, we have ignored the existence of the public authorities—local and national governments—as receivers and payers out of money, and we have ignored also the possibility that the economy may have imports from and exports to the rest of the world. Once these complications are admitted, the pattern of flow becomes as shown in Diagram 2. Households now, in addition to the transactions mentioned before, pay personal taxes to the public authorities and receive from them what are generally called 'transfer payments'—that is to say, payments such as national insurance benefits, public assistance, and interest on the national debt which are not returns for any service they are currently rendering. The public authorities are, of course, also large employers, buying services from households, just as enterprises do. Enterprises, similarly, pay taxes to the government and also receive payment from it for the goods and services which it buys from them. They also buy from and sell to the outside world—it is convenient to ignore for this purpose the transactions which households and public authorities have directly with other countries. The role of the capital market is now complicated by the possibility that the public authorities may contribute savings to it, or may, on the other hand, be net borrowers from it, as enterprises usually are; the outside world may also borrow from or lend to it but we need not trouble about that at present. Once again, it may be noted in passing that the condition for maintaining a constant flow of goods and services at constant prices is that there should be no net leakage of money out of or into active circulation. This time, however, money may leak into, or from, not only the capital market, but also the rest of the world. The savings of households, enterprises, and the government may equal expenditure by enterprises on fixed investment, but there may be an excess of imports over exports, so that money is flowing out of the country's active circulation, not into its capital market, but into the hands of foreigners. It is when the internal and the external leakage add up to zero that the conditions for a constant flow of money in the economy are satisfied.

Of course, the picture which has been sketched of the flow of money payments in an exchange economy is still grossly over-simplified in certain respects. In particular, it completely ignores the enormous volume of transactions between one enterprise and another. In connection with the production of a particular suit of clothes, for instance, there will have been paid out not only the price of the imported raw material and the rewards for the various factors of production in the country which went to manufacture and merchant it, but also a series of payments— from the topmaker to the wool-merchant, from the spinner to the topmaker, the weaver to the spinner, the tailor to the weaver, and perhaps other stages as well—which may add up to more than the value of the finished suit. In principle, it would be possible to draw a huge diagram (or compile a huge table) distinguishing not only households as a whole from enterprises as a whole, but every enterprise from every other, so that inter-enterprise payments could be recorded. In practice, such tables have, in fact, been drawn up which distinguish a very large number of industrial groups (as many as two hundred), recording estimates of the payments which every one makes to and receives from every other one, as well as to (and from) households, the government, and the outside world. They provide the most detailed summaries of the anatomy of an economy which have so far been made, and are of great use in making it possible to predict the effects upon each industry separately of changes in demand for particular kinds of goods. For the present purpose, however, we need only note that this very large volume of inter-enterprise payments exists, and that more money payments are therefore necessary to finance a given output of goods and services that one might suppose merely from examining Diagram 2.

Money Flow as a Measure of Income
Having before us a picture of the main money flows in an economy where all goods and services produced are sold for money, we are in a position to make a measurement of the total money value of all the goods and services produced in a unit period of time. In order to do this, it is necessary first to sort out from Diagram 2

those classes of payment which correspond to the total value of output. It is not very hard to see that this can be done in more than one way. In the first place, there are certain streams of payment represented in the diagram which are the final payments for finished goods and services by the people or authorities which are going to use or consume them. Consumption expenditure by households clearly comes into this class, so do public authorities' expenditures on goods and services, and so, again, do purchases of producers' durable goods by enterprises. To these we must add inventory investment; the money value of increases in stocks of goods. On the other hand, not all of these goods and services have been produced in the economy in question; if we wish to confine ourselves to those which have, we must deduct imports. We have, however, so far omitted those goods and services which are produced in the economy, but sold outside it, namely exports, and these must be added in. We have now included all the payments made by the final buyers for goods and services actually produced in the economy—the total value of its gross income or product when all the goods and services are valued at market prices. It consists of:

Consumers' expenditure + private investment expenditure + public expenditure on goods and services + exports − imports.

In the second place, however, it is clear that we ought to be able to arrive at the total value of the goods and services produced in the economy by adding up the sums paid by enterprises for the factors of production used in producing them. It looks at first sight as if the two items 'factor payments' made by enterprises to households and 'wages and salaries paid by public authorities' to households would do for this; a little thought shows however, that this is not the whole story. Part of the total value of goods and services produced by enterprises is not paid out in wages, salaries, profits, etc., but, although it forms part of profits, is put to reserve instead of being distributed as dividend. This is the item which appears in the diagram as 'enterprises' savings'. If we add it to factor payments by enterprises and public authorities the result is the total reward imputed to all the factors of production in the country for their productive effort, including that part which is not actually paid to them in money, but saved up on their behalf. It will not, however, correspond to the previous total— the gross national product at market prices—because what is actually paid for the national output in the market includes taxes (such as purchase tax and the excise duties on beer and tobacco) which go to the government, not to the suppliers of factors of production. Or, to put it in another way, what is actually received by enterprises for their output includes not only what they pay to (or save on behalf of) the suppliers of factors of production but also what they have to pay to the government in taxation. The total of factor payments and enterprises' savings is therefore described as the economy's 'gross product at factor cost', and to convert it into the gross product at market prices it is necessary to add on enterprises' tax payments. (If the government pays subsidies to enterprises, which tend to reduce the market prices of their output below factor cost, just as taxes on enterprises tend to do the opposite, then these subsidies must be deducted from enterprises' tax payments in making this adjustment.)

In Chapter 2, the gross product or income of an economy was thought of—or, at least, the attempt was made to think of it—simply as a heterogeneous stream of goods and services. It now emerges that, in a market economy, it is practicable to measure the total money value of the goods and services which flow down this stream in whatever unit period we choose—usually a year. This is, clearly, the only way of measuring the flow of income or product by a single number which looks like having any useful meaning at all. It would be impossible to measure the amount of goods and services concerned by any physical dimension —such as their weight—and quite meaningless for economic purposes to do so even if the composition of income were so far simplified that such a physical measure became practicable. Does the money value of income or product really have any meaning, however? Does it make sense to add together the values of power stations and cheese and medical services produced during the year?

The values of these finished goods and services are, as we have just seen, equal to the payments made for factors of production used in producing them—if we ignore the adjustment needed to change the product reckoned at factor cost into that reckoned at market prices. If there were only one factor of production—say labour of uniform quality—we would have no hesitation in saying that the money value of a good or service which enters into the economy's product was a satisfactory measure of the amount of the community's basic resources (labour in this case) which is put into it, and we would therefore take the aggregate value of all the goods and services produced as being a good measure of the resources used in producing them. In fact, of course, it is not so simple as that; the basic resources of the community consist of many different kinds of labour, earning different wages and salaries, as well as of capital and natural resources of many kinds. Although this is not the place to attempt a full answer to these questions, it may be said at once that there are two respects in which it makes sense to add up the money values of different kinds of commodity, where it would not make sense to add up, say, their volumes or weights (if they have any). In the first place, the relative values of different commodities in a market economy reflect in an important sense the relative amounts of the community's basic resources which have gone into producing them, and their aggregate value therefore serves as a reasonably good measure of the aggregate resources which they embody. In the second place, the relative values of different things bears some relation to their relative want-satisfying power. If a pencil and a loaf of bread sell for the same price, to the same people, there is a presumption that they satisfy wants of about the same urgency. If they do not, if, for instance the want satisfied by the bread were decidedly the more urgent, then the people in question would be open to the charge of laying out their money unwisely—they would do better to divert some of their expenditure from pencils to bread. That is not to say, of course, that the total value of a community's income is a measure of its satisfaction in it, or of the extent to which its wants are satisfied by it. It cannot be properly said that a man whose income is £1,000 a year (i.e. who is able to buy goods and services to that value) is twice as well off, or has twice as much satisfaction from his income, as he would have if his income was only £500. But £1 worth of one commodity has about the same want-satisfying power (especially if its use is spread over a substantial period, such as a year) as £1 worth of another—unless there is a presumption that, like caviare and margarine, they are bought by people whose wants are already satisfied to markedly different extents. Without going into this rather complicated matter any further, therefore, we may say that the money value of an economy's income is a measure of its magnitude which has considerable validity. We must, however, be careful to note that comparisons made in value terms between the incomes of different economies, or between the incomes enjoyed by one economy at different times, can be made only so long as the prices at which the things composing the incomes in question are valued are the same in both economies or at both times.

Money Payments and the Money Supply
From this short digression on the significance which this particular

money flow—the money value of an economy's income—has for the economist, we may now return to look at its relation to other money flows and at the relation of the total money flow to the stock of money which the community needs.

In the United Kingdom, in 1956, the gross national product at market prices was, in round figures, £20,600 million (made up of consumers' expenditure £13,700 m., public expenditure on current goods and services £3,500 m., and gross investment, £3,400 m., with a small excess of exports over imports). In the course of producing and distributing goods and services to this total market value, the main streams of payment between the sectors of the economy distinguished in Diagram 2 (excluding imports and exports) amounted to about £45,000 million. It may be roughly estimated that the payments between enterprises, and between the central and local governments, were probably somewhere between £30,000 and £35,000 million. The total payments which were in some way connected with the production and distribution of the national product were thus, altogether, about four times as great as the value of that product. It must be added that there are other categories of payments which have less direct connection with the production and distribution of the national product, such as dealings in securities on the stock exchange and the operations of the Treasury in connection with the national debt. It is a surprising, but inescapable, fact that these 'financial' payments amount to something like four times as much as all the others together. They may be thought of as payments within the money market. They are, however, extremely localized—mostly within the square mile of the City of London—and the amount of money actually used in carrying them out is surprisingly small. It is permissible to ignore them when considering the relation between the total amount of money and the payments which are connected with the production and distribution of goods and services.

The money by means of which these transactions are carried out in a modern community is of various kinds. It is not appropriate, however, to go into fine distinctions here, nor to consider the interesting historical process by which money has come to assume its modern forms. For all practical purposes, anything can be counted as money which is normally and generally used and accepted in the country with which one is concerned as a means of payment. In modern economies, such means of payment take two main forms; notes and coin on the one hand, and bank deposits, which can be used to make payments by writing a cheque, on the other. In the United Kingdom, the United States, and Australia, for example, bank deposits of this kind constitute more than three-quarters of the money of both kinds together; in France, Germany, Italy, and Sweden, on the other hand, they make up only about half the total money supply. Roughly speaking, notes and coin serve as money partly because they are 'legal tender' —that is to say, in law they are regarded as adequate means of paying debts—and partly because people are used to them. Bank deposits transferrable by cheque serve as money because they are extremely convenient to the payer, especially for making large payments, and because, in the circles where they are mainly used, the persons who accept them usually know enough about the payers to trust that they have deposits in the bank from which the cheque can be met—as well as trusting the bank to have cash on hand with which to meet the cheque if they should want payment ultimately in notes and coin.

How much money is required to make possible a given volume of transactions can be seen to depend upon the way in which the transactions in question are distributed through the year. Take, for instance, an imaginary economy without any complications from saving and investment, public finance, or foreign trade, in which all the enterprises pay for their factors of production every Friday, and the households pay their earnings back to the enterprises in return for goods and services during the following week. If the households have, indeed, spent up by Friday morning, and the enterprises have no money in hand on Friday night, the economy will be able to manage all its transactions with a sum of money equal to one week's income. Similarly, if factors of production were paid monthly instead of weekly, a supply of money equal to a month's income would be needed. How much money an economy needs is therefore very closely connected with the frequency of payments for factors of production—which in practice range from weekly (for wages) to once a year (for some interest and dividend payments), averaging perhaps something like once a fortnight. It also depends on the timing of households' expenditures; whether, and to what extent, they save up part of their income over a number of pay-days to buy clothes or radios or cars, and, to some extent, on how soon after pay-day their regular expenditure mainly happens. It must be remembered, also, that payments for factors of production and household expenditure are together not much more than half the total non-financial payments of the economy; the remainder, consisting mainly of payments between enterprises, also require the use of money to an extent which depends on the same general considerations as have just been discussed—their frequency and the way in which receipts and expenditures fit together.

There is some evidence that, both in the United Kingdom and in the United States, the amount of money that is used regularly for transactions connected with the production and distribution of goods and services amounts to about two months' income for the whole economy. The total amount of money existing in these, and most other highly developed economies is, however, very much greater than that. For the United States, United Kingdom, France, Italy, and Australia, for instance, it was in 1953 about four months' income, though markedly less in Japan, Germany, and Sweden. The excess of the total supply of money over the amount regularly needed for transactions consists, of course, of the sums which people find it convenient to hold to meet an emergency, or of those parts of their saved-up wealth which they have not seen fit to invest in securities or other income-yielding property, perhaps because the cost and trouble of investing is too great, or perhaps because they are afraid of such securities or property being low in price at the (probably indefinite) future time when they might want to sell them. The point to note is that these quantities of money in most highly-developed modern economies are large—the total supply of money for all purposes is usually very generous in relation to the requirements of industry and trade alone. That, however, does not mean that plenty of money is always available for people who would like to expand their payments in connection with production, investment, or consumption. The money market does not manage to make by any means all the money which is lying idle available for spenders even at a price, and the price (in interest) which would be necessary to get some of it is also no doubt high. Although the banks and other monetary authorities, which are able to create money, generally adjust their supply to a large extent in conformity with the demands which are made on them for genuine purposes of industry or trade, they have it in their power—and sometimes exercise the power—to put a curb on spending, and thus on the volume of production, even when the total supply of the money in the economy might look, in the light of the foregoing discussion, ample to finance the regular payments required by production and distribution.

We can now sum up. In an exchange economy, where every good and service produced is exchanged for money, the basic part of the machinery by which the system works is a circular flow of money, from productive enterprises to the households of the people who provide the factors of production, and back again. This flow is somewhat complicated by saving, by the financial activities of the government, and by foreign trade. When the flows of money and of commodities in the economy are steady, the purchase of goods for investment of any kind is financed by the savings which flow into the money market from households, enterprises, or the public authorities. The condition of the maintenance of a steady flow is that any excess of saving over investment within the country should be balanced by an excess of exports over imports. If such a balance does not exist, the flow of money will either expand or contract, with parallel effects on the volume of production and/or the level of prices, so that economic activity and the price level are bound up with the flow of money.

How much money is required to run an exchange economy with a given level of production and prices depends on the pattern of payments, their frequency and how they happen to interlock, and also on how much money people want to hold for purposes other than transactions connected with goods and services. In modern economies, such transactions seem to be equal to about four times the value of goods and services produced (the gross national product, which can be identified with certain combinations of the main streams of payment); the minimum amount of money needed to keep them going is perhaps about two months' gross national product, but the actual supply of money held in many modern economies is equal to about four months' gross product. The total amount of money has some effect, though not always a very clear one, upon the flows, and so upon production and price-levels.

With this glance at the most essential elements in the structure of any economy and at the machinery of exchange, where exchange has become universal, we may now turn to what may be regarded as the key questions about the performance of an economy—how much it produces, and what kinds of living it provides.

CHAPTER 4

High and Low Productivity

HOW good or poor a living a family or an economy gets depends, immediately, on two things—how much it produces, and at what prices it can exchange it for the things it wants. Both of these vary enormously, especially between one country and another. Since the first is in some ways easier to understand, and is also in some degree a cause of the second, it is convenient to look at them in the order in which they have just been mentioned—variations in productiveness first.

Farm Incomes and Decreasing Returns
Nowhere is variation in productiveness more important than in agriculture, and there are not many branches of production in which it is more striking than there. The most comprehensive calculation which brings out these differences is a famous one by Mr Colin Clark, relating to the years just before the war. Taking all the agricultural products of a large number of countries, valuing them at a set of uniform world market prices, and subtracting the similarly valued fertilizers, feeding stuffs, and other materials used up in the course of production, he obtained, in value terms, assessments of the total products attributable to the agricultural populations (together with their land and equipment) in those countries. From these he worked out estimates of production per man engaged in agriculture. Translating his results roughly into the present (1958) British prices, we see that output per man ranged all the way from between £25 and £50 worth in India, China, Egypt, and the Philippines to £500-£1,000 worth in Australia, New Zealand, and Argentina. In the poorest countries (agriculturally) a farmer produced only about a fortieth, or at best a twentieth, as much as one in some of the most favoured parts of the world. The difference has probably widened somewhat since then. To put it in another way, a farming family in Australia, New Zealand, or in some of the more favoured parts of the Americas, can feed itself and from six to a dozen other families very well; a typical Indian or Chinese farming family, even if it did not have to sell any of its produce, would fare only very

plainly at the best, and the worst would not always be even adequately nourished.

This comparison is not really quite fair. The Indian or Chinese farmer works with very little equipment indeed; the Australian or American farmer is helped by a great deal of equipment—farm buildings, tractors, and other machinery—which are made, and probably maintained, by other people. The contribution of the people in other industries who supply these things should really be subtracted to get at the productivity of the people actually on the farms, or else the total product should be divided, not by the number of farmers alone, but by that number *plus* the makers of agricultural machinery, the people who provide fuel for agricultural tractors, and so forth. This would reduce the contrast in productivity between agriculturalists in the most favoured and the least favoured countries, but not really by very much; when all allowances were made, it would still be an enormous one.

What are the reasons for these differences? One has just been mentioned—differences in the amount of mechanical equipment—but two others, in some degree connected with it, are perhaps even more striking; namely, differences in the amount (and quality) of land which each farmer has at his disposal, and differences in knowledge about farming methods. The differences in amount of land available can be measured, and turn out to be enormous. The amount of land actually used for farming purposes (cultivated or used as pasture) per man working on it varies from something like 350 acres in Australia and Argentina, to less than three acres in Japan (it was about 35 acres for each man in the United Kingdom before the war and about 100 acres in the United States). But such a calculation may not mean very much; there is a big variation in quality of land and, still more, of climate. A heroic attempt to get over this difficulty was made by Mr Clark, who, taking technical advice from climatologists, reduced the area of each country for which he could get statistics to terms of what he called 'standard farm land'—excluding all the uninhabited deserts, dividing the area of semi-desert, for instance (like much of the Australian sheep country), by 100 and making corresponding adjustments for land with other types of climate. With these corrections the picture is considerably altered, but the differences of natural endowment, now more faithfully reflected, are still shown to be very great. Australia, New Zealand, and Canada have, on this reckoning, the equivalent of more than 250 acres of 'standard' land (not all of it at present used) for each man in agriculture; Egypt and Palestine have only two or four acres, and

India and China something like ten and six respectively. The United States still has about 100 acres; the United Kingdom about 50.

The relation between land per man and production per man, which these calculations bring out, is roughly in accordance with a very simple generalization, namely, that with a given agricultural labour force, farm production varies in proportion to the square root of the amount of land. The relation is only a very rough one, and there are important departures from it. Indeed, the estimate of the amount of 'standard' land per man is so imperfect that it would be surprising (and suspicious) if an exact relation were to be found. Moreover, while the amount of equipment, which clearly affect production, is not specifically taken into account in this calculation, its effect creeps in by the back door, in as much as the countries where there is most land per man tend on the whole to be those which have most equipment too—indeed, the possibility of cultivating a large area per man obviously depends on such machinery as tractors and combine harvesters. In the same way, plenty of equipment often (but not always) goes with a fairly high level of knowledge of farming methods and good facilities for applying it. At any rate, one finds all three of these—land, equipment, and knowledge—at high levels in certain countries such as the United States, Canada, Australia, and New Zealand, while, at the other end of the scale, in India and China, all three are scarce.

It is not easy to separate out the effects of these three factors making for high productivity, but it can, at any rate, be seen that knowledge and equipment can make up for shortage of land within limits. Danish and Dutch farmers produce two or three times as much as those in parts of eastern Europe where the amount of land they each have and the natural advantages of soil and climate are not, on balance, very different. They achieve this by practising an entirely different system of agriculture which demands more technical knowledge, more organization, more equipment, and much more capital in the form of livestock, and which, incidentally, makes up for the shortage of land partly by feeding cattle on imported feeding stuffs for which they pay, in part, with meat and dairy products. The productivity of Japanese farmers more than doubled in the first forty years of this century almost entirely through the use of better methods (not requiring much extra equipment), and the Japanese method of rice cultivation is now being introduced into India with impressive results. Land, equipment, and knowledge go together to bring about high output per man, but they can be put together in widely differing proportions. Because of the difficulty of measuring any of them (especially the impossibility of measuring knowledge), there is no precise formula showing how output depends on all three of them together, but there clearly is a relation of dependence in which shortage of one factor can be compensated for by abundance of the others.

All these facts are entirely in accordance with the famous 'law of diminishing returns', which has earned so much odium for economists among people who have misunderstood it. In its simplest form, the law simply says that the less land you have per head, the less you will produce per head, supposing that your supply of equipment, knowledge, and any other aids to production is not increased. (It applies equally to the effects of shortage of equipment per head if the supply of natural resources, knowledge, and other aids does not increase.) This has sometimes been taken as implying a prediction that as population increases (the supply of land and other natural resources in the country concerned, or in the world, being, of course, unchanged, or, at any rate, not increased), output per head, at least in agriculture, must fall. In fact, it does nothing of the sort. Especially in the last century or so, the amount of equipment and fertilizers, and knowledge about plant and animal breeding and feeding have increased enormously, and so have knowledge and equipment connected with transport, so that vast areas of land—all the west and middle west of North America, and much of the interiors of the other continents—have become accessible and so farmable. The prospects and effects of these favourable changes may have been sometimes underestimated by economists thinking of the law of diminishing returns, but that the increase of knowledge and equipment have outweighed the increasing scarcity of land in relation to people living on it in most parts of the world, and for the world taken as a whole, during this period of time, does not in the least affect the truth or usefulness of the law. As we have seen, it is a generalization which can safely be made from evidence about farm areas, farm populations, and farm production in the world today, the difficulties of measurement (and the impossibility of directly measuring differences in technical knowledge) notwithstanding. Alternatively, if we are prepared to accept the 'law' as a self-evident, or at least highly plausible, statement about production in general, we may say that it goes quite a long way towards 'explaining' the differences in average agricultural production per person on the farms in different countries.

D

Manufacture and Mechanism

In manufacturing industry, once again, the differences in productiveness between people in different countries are striking, but they are rather harder to interpret than the corresponding differences, which have just been glanced at, in agricultural productiveness. Perhaps somewhere about half the people in the world who 'manufacture'—that is to say, make things with their hands—work in factories, the other half being craftsmen or labourers who work in their own homes, or in small workshops, or in industries like building where the work is done out of doors, or, at any rate, not under factory conditions. So far as factory work is concerned, the diversity between average national levels of production per person immediately engaged in it is very much less than in agriculture. Mr Clark estimates that output per person working in factories in the United States is about seven times as great as for the corresponding people in India, these being the most and least productive countries in this respect with substantial factory industries for which the necessary statistics were available. Factory industry, however, is generally very much more productive in relation to the people employed in it than non-factory industry making the same kind of product. A handloom weaver, of whom there are still a great many in the East, may 'produce' in a day only a fifteenth of the amount of cloth produced by a weaver in a modern mill. A spinner in a modern mill may produce a hundred times as much yarn a day as a skilled man (or, more usually, woman) with a spinning wheel. In industries which are necessarily non-factory (like road-making), mechanical methods are obviously very much more productive, in this simple sense, than non-mechanical. A man with a bulldozer can move hundreds of times as much earth in a day as a man with a shovel.

These ways in which mechanical and factory methods 'save' direct labour are familiar to everyone now. Machines are direct substitutes for human hands and muscles in a great many operations. They are often superior substitutes in that they can be made to perform more accurately, or more quickly, or more continuously, or with the application of greater force than a labourer or craftsman. Moreover, mechanical sources of energy— steam engines, internal combustion engines, and water turbines— make available a very abundant substitute for some or all of the human muscle-power which is otherwise necessary for all manufacturing and building operations. The horse-power of the engines and electric motors used in factory industry is, in the United Kingdom, rather over three, and in the United States over seven for each person employed. It is generally reckoned that a man doing hard physical labour has a power (rate of doing work) averaging about a tenth of a horse-power over the whole working day. It follows, therefore, that machines supply from thirty to seventy times as much energy in the factories of a modern economy as could be provided by the muscles of the people who work in those factories.

A good deal of the advantage of a factory system obviously comes from this source, though cheap and widespread electric power makes it possible for people who work in their own homes or in small workshops to have mechanical power as well. But, quite apart from their connection with elaborate machinery and mechanical power, factories provide another advantage. They enable the jobs which are still done by hand—the operating and feeding of machines, and the assembly, inspection, and testing of products, for instance—to be so organized that most workers can specialize on a small and simple operation. This makes it easy and quick to train them, saves the time that is always lost when people go from one phase to another of a complicated task (especially if they have to change their position very much in the process), and reduces fatigue by enabling the work to become rhythmic and automatic. Experience shows that the perils of monotony and boredom can be avoided if care is taken, and that the gains in productivity per head which flow from 'work simplification' of this kind—which is practicable only where people work together in quite large teams—is enormous. The famous pin-factory about which Adam Smith wrote 180 years ago remains an excellent example of this.

Two other advantages of factory production should perhaps be mentioned in passing. As compared with production in small scattered workshops, or the 'putting out' of work to people in their own homes, it greatly diminishes the handling and carrying about of materials and products in small lots, enabling them to be moved economically by the truckload or on conveyor belts. And, finally, there is the possibility of using a staff of experts to smooth and improve the method and organization of production, and to apply new technical knowledge—even the most tradition-bound factory establishment being, on the whole, easier to change than a scattered body of independent craftsmen.

So far as output per person immediately engaged in producing a particular kind of good is concerned, therefore, the superiority of factory industry over handicraft methods is both very great and easy to understand. It is also, however, rather misleading, for a

reason similar to one which was noted in connection with agriculture. The total labour which is concerned in, say, producing cotton cloth from raw cotton is not simply that which is employed in the cotton mills. Machinery and industrial buildings, not to mention power, are not provided ready-made by nature, and the labour involved in making them available in the right form and the right place has to be taken into the reckoning. The gain in production from mechanical methods is not to be reckoned by simply comparing what the users of machinery can produce with what they could have produced without it; we have to compare a community of non-mechanized producers with a mechanized community which maintains and powers its plant and machines and replaces them with new ones as they wear out. In manfacturing industry, however, this qualification is not so important as one might expect. Industrial buildings, plant and machinery do not, on the average, cost very much in relation to their output—often less than twice the value of the products that flow from them in a year; the annual cost of keeping them in order is normally only a few per cent. of their original cost, and they last a good many years (on average) before they have to be renewed. Modern industry, as a whole, devotes less than ten per cent. of its efforts to keeping its plant and equipment in order and renewing it as that becomes necessary. It does, however, happen with some very heavily mechanized industries that the average amount of work which has to be done outside them to maintain and replace their equipment is actually greater than that which is done inside them in operating it—the electricity industry is an example. It is therefore necessary to be careful in estimating the labour-saving, or productivity-increasing, power of industrial machinery.

But, when all is said and done, this power is enormous. With all allowances made for maintenance and replacement of machinery, provision of power, administration, and the other indirect calls for manpower which factory production makes, it is probably, on the average over a representative range of products, at least ten times as productive per hour of total labour involved as were the handicrafts practised nearly everywhere at the beginning of last century, and still practised in many places today. There are, of course, many products which have never been made, and probably never would have been made, except by methods which are, in some sense, highly mechanized—this is especially true, for instance, of things involving aluminium and other light metals, or any of a great variety of chemical products, which need a great deal of electrical energy, or in some cases very high pressures, to produced them at all—or, at any rate, to produce them as other than laboratory curiosities.

Within factory industry itself, however, there are very considerable differences between one country and another—it has been mentioned earlier that output per person directly employed in American factories is about seven times as great as than in Indian factories. The United Kingdom and western Europe generally came about half-way between these extremes. The allowances for labour involved indirectly in maintaining, replacing, and powering machinery and plant would modify these contrasts a little, but not very much.

The reasons for these differences in industrial productivity between countries have attracted a great deal of attention in recent years. A considerable part of the immediate reason seems to be that American industry uses more powerful and elaborate machinery than (for instance) British—it has already been remarked that the horse-power of the machinery used is more than twice as great in relation to the number of people employed in the former as in the latter. But while this, so far as it goes, is a satisfactory explanation, one naturally wants to know why British industry is less highly mechanized than American. Is it that American industry got ahead through some historical accident and that British industry, while able to follow the same path with equal advantage, has not yet caught up? Or is there some reason which prevents British industry from developing the same highly mechanized techniques as American industry?

The Conditions of Mechanization

These turn out to be deep questions. Some writers have thought that it pays American industry to be more mechanized than it would pay British industry to be because American industry is on a much larger scale—it has a very much bigger market and some very big firms. But in most industries the number of people employed in the typical American factory (which is more likely to matter than the number employed by the typical firm, possibly with several factories), is not very different from the corresponding number in Britain, and the industries where it is most markedly larger are not uniformly those where American superiority in mechanization and output per man are greatest. It looks at first sight as if the size of the whole market for a product may explain rather more; the American market is most markedly bigger than the British in some industries (such as motors and wireless) where mechanization and productivity are also most markedly superior.

But superior American industrial productivity goes back to a time when the total American market was a good deal smaller than the British.

It does, however, seem to be the case that American production of any particular model or variety of manufactured good is on a much larger scale than in Britain, and that this is quite an important factor in raising productivity. Most products are more standardized in America; there are fewer varieties of them altogether than in Britain, and any particular factory will probably be making a smaller number of different models. Thus, production of any one model can be planned on a larger scale, which means that it is more worth while to set up automatic or semi-automatic machinery to make it.

Why there should be this difference between the United States and Britain (or Europe generally) is clearly the next question, and the answer to it may be in some degree psychological or sociological rather than economic. But one important contributory factor may well be an economic one—namely, that American communities grew very rapidly both in numbers and in wealth at the time when industrial production was first developing on a large scale (from about 1870 onwards). There were many immigrants entirely unused to the standard of living which the country could provide, and many native Americans who went west across the continent, or who moved up rapidly into more comfortable circumstances. Altogether, therefore, there were many people who had not become set in habits of buying particular kinds of goods, or were willing to change, and thus could be persuaded to take standardized goods which were cheap to produce. At the same time, the very rapid expansion of the market must have encouraged firms to launch out in producing quantity rather than variety.

Another frequently met explanation for the growth of highly mechanized production in the United States, and other countries where it has developed very strongly is that in these countries labour is dear, and that it therefore pays to use more nearly automatic machinery instead. To this there is a serious objection. Machinery is, after all, produced partly by labour. Should not dear labour therefore mean that machinery will be dear, too? In so far as this is a valid objection, it implies that the countries where it pays especially well to use machinery instead of labour will be not simply those where labour is dear in general, but those where the labour or other resources used in producing machinery are specially cheap (or efficient) in comparison with those used for producing other things. In such a country, the natural resources that go into the metal-making and engineering industries may be specially plentiful and accessible, or engineering skill and knowledge may be abundant, or there may be few people who are either more able or more willing to do the heavy labouring which goes with less mechanized industry than the lighter semi-skilled work characteristic of high mechanization. All these conditions seem to apply—and to have applied for some time—to the United States. Natural resources favour the production of metals and power, general and technical education are good, and for a long time many of the men who might otherwise have been labourers in industry went to help push the agricultural frontier further west.

So far as Britain is concerned, there is another circumstance which helps to make a simple copying of highly mechanized American methods inappropriate, namely, that people are reluctant to work machinery as intensively as is usual in the United States. There are some expenses connected with machinery and plant which are more or less independent of the intensity with which they are used—rent of buildings, interest on capital, and maintenance against the weather, for instance. Even more important than these, in some industries, is the fact that a particular kind of machine, or the product it produces, may be expected to be out of date in a few years. Whether it is worth setting up an elaborate, labour-saving plant, therefore depends to a considerable extent on how much can be got out of it, not just during the whole time for which it might be made to last, but within quite a short time. It is an important fact, therefore, that American workers are more willing than British to allow double shift working in some industries (textiles, for instance) and that British workers are in some cases inclined to insist upon a rather easier working pace.

It is important to make due allowance for these differences between countries which make the most appropriate degrees of mechanization in industry differ from one another. But, when all is said and done, the main differences in productivity are due not to any permanent diversity of conditions, but simply to the fact that different countries are at very different stages on the road of industrial development. Progress along this road may be slow. Not only must the machinery and buildings of the factories themselves be accumulated, but an adequate transport system has to be built up for carrying raw materials and products about in bulk—a job usually much bigger than building and equipping factories. People have to be trained in the skills required for factory work, including the very high skills needed for designing plant or products and operating the more complex pieces of plant such as generating stations or oil refineries. It is true that equipment and people with special skills can be brought into a country from abroad, but the extent to which this can be afforded is, naturally, not unlimited, and much is bound in any case to depend on the skills and attitudes of the people of the country itself.

These considerations set limits to the rate at which elaborate and highly mechanized methods of industrial production can be introduced into a country, supposing that the government, or other sufficiently wealthy and powerful groups, are determined to introduce them. But the industrial developments of many countries has been held up most of all not so much by technical limitations on the rate of progress as by the absence of anyone with both the will and the means to bring it about at all. Governments often either consider that technical development is not their concern, or are not well enough provided with administrative ability, technical advice, or sources of money to do much about it. Private business-men often lack knowledge of the opportunities for producing better or more cheaply by mechanical methods, and, what is perhaps more important, they lack the large amounts of money needed to build and equip factories, and to set up organizations for selling goods which have been produced in bulk. Means of transporting raw materials and finished goods cheaply to and from factories are also lacking in many countries; it has not been thought worth while to build adequate roads and railways because there was little traffic, and there could not be traffic because there were no roads or railways to take it.

To a large extent, also, it is true in economically undeveloped countries that it would not pay to set up mechanized production of any single type of good by itself, because labour is so cheap that hand methods are no more expensive. We have just seen that this argument, as it stands, is not a very good one in relation to countries which are already highly industrialized, because, there, if labour is cheap, that very fact should tend to make machinery cheap as well. But in non-industrialized countries, machinery-producing industries do not exist (they generally come rather late in the course of development), so that the only machinery obtainable is that imported from industrialized countries where labour is relatively dear. It is only as labour becomes dearer in general, or becomes more efficient in the machine-producing industries in relation to other activities that the case for mechanization gathers strength, and both of these changes are largely products of mechanization. The process of mechanization is in this way (and in others as well) one which tends to gather strength as it goes along, like a rolled snowball. This is all of a piece with its being weak in its early stages, and often difficult to start at all, and helps to explain why we find different countries at such very different stages on a path of development which is so advantageous to all of them that one might, at first sight, think it surprising that they are not all racing neck and neck along it.

Coolies, Ships, and Services
Something has now been said about the differences in productiveness in both agriculture and manufacturing industry. It remains to consider the other activities in the economy, which are often lumped together under the heading 'tertiary production' or 'service industries'. They are, of course, a very mixed bag, including such things as transport, the professions, the entertainment industry, hotels, and domestic service. From this list, transport clearly stands out as the industry in which the benefits of mechanization are most obvious; as obvious, indeed, as they are in manufacturing. The whole body of people responsible directly and indirectly for running a railway system, including the miners who produce the coal, the men who maintain the track and equipment, and an allowance for the complete replacement of the whole system as it wears out, provide at least a hundred times and perhaps two hundred times as many ton-miles of transport service per man as coolies could give. Ocean shipping is even more efficient in this sense, the number of ton-miles of transport provided per person directly and indirectly involved (including those who produce the ships, the fuel, and the port facilities) being about ten times as great as on the railways. Aircraft, purely as load-carriers, are still relatively inefficient; the average ton-miles per man directly and indirectly engaged, calculated on the same basis as for railways, seems to be only a tenth or a twentieth of what the latter provide.

The advantage to an economy with modern means of transport is therefore clear, especially when one considers what a great amount of transport service enters into the total goods and services used. In the big, wealthy economies, such as the United Kingdom and the United States, something between 6,000 and 11,000 ton-miles of goods transport a year is required for each inhabitant; for the world as a whole, the average is probably between 1,500 and 2,000 ton-miles. The difference between the amount of human effort required to provide a given amount of transport in (say) China, which is still very poorly provided with modern means of communication, and in western Europe, or North America, is obviously immense; a difference partly responsible for the far smaller amount of transport services which the poorer countries use as compared with the more highly developed parts of the world.

Between countries fairly well provided with modern means of transport, also, there are considerable differences in the productiveness of the people directly and indirectly engaged; here, again the United States seems to be ahead of most other countries. The differences, however, are small in comparison with those between the countries with good roads and railways and those without. Such as they are, they seem to be connected mainly with two factors—the extent to which the carrying capacity of the transport system is used, and the average distance over which things have to be moved. Since modern transport systems require a lot of effort and expense to keep them in order, even if they are only lightly used, the amount of labour per unit of service provided is generally less if the equipment is used to something near its full capacity. And, since much of the labour connected with transport is concerned with loading, unloading, shunting, sorting, and the like, rather than with simply moving vehicles along roads, rails, or water routes, the average amount of labour per ton-mile of service tends to be lowest where the average length of haul is high. The great efficiency of the United States railways, in particular, seems to be due to a combination of fairly heavy use of the lines and a long average length of haul—by the same token the Russian railways should be outstandingly efficient in terms of labour, or cost, per ton-mile, but no direct statistics are available to confirm this.

When we pass from transport to the other 'service' industries, there are far less obvious reasons for differences in the productiveness of labour from one country to another. It is true that, in some countries, professional skills are much scarcer than in others, that in some there is relatively little tradition of honesty in administration or commerce, and that there are considerable differences between countries in the effort and enthusiasm with which people work. In particular fields we see great differences; much of the office work which enters into administration and commerce is just beginning to be revolutionized by electronic machinery, which will no doubt be applied in some countries much sooner than in others. The differences between the efficiencies with which labour is used in, say, an American 'supermarket' and an African market are also very great. But the big differences in level of mechanical equipment and in endowment of natural resources, which affect productiveness so strongly in manufacturing, transport, and agriculture, do not generally operate with anything like the same force in such fields as administration, shopkeeping, catering, or housework.

Why Prices matter, too

So much, then, for variations in physical productiveness between different countries. It is obvious that, if we compare two countries which are both wholly or mainly self-sufficient—that is to say, each produces all or nearly all of the goods and services that it uses—we are bound to find that the average real incomes per head in them will be proportional to some sort of average of the outputs per head in the different branches of economic activity. If one produces twice as much per hour worked in every occupation as the other does, then the real income earned per hour worked will, on the average, be twice as high in the first country as in the second. In this highly simplified case, the relation between physical productivity and standard of living is clear.

The real world, however, is very much too complicated for such a simple example to give us anything like a full understanding of the differences in standard of living that we actually find. For one thing, we cannot explain the differences even in average standards of living of nations, still less the differences between smaller communities, or between families, simply in terms of their physical productivities, because they do not all produce the same things. How, on a basis of productivity can we explain the difference between the livings of a community that produces mainly machinery and vehicles, and one that produces mainly bacon and butter? To do this, we clearly need additional information about the prices of the things produced. Again, different communities do not all consume the same things—or, even if they do, they do not buy these same (or similar) goods and services in the same markets. One community eats a lot of meat, another very little; even though they both buy services, one may buy them at a high price, another at a low one. To explain differences between standards of living, therefore, we need to explain not only differences in productivity, but also prices—both the prices of the goods and services which people produce (so that we may know the money value of the income) and the prices of the goods and services they consume (so that we can see how far their income goes). We must now turn, therefore, to some reflections on the determination of prices.

CHAPTER 5

What Determines Prices?

THE first point to strike anyone who looks around the world to see how prices seem to be determined would, surely, be that there are many different kinds of price, determined in many different ways. Some prices, to start with, are deliberately fixed by an authority or a firm. The prices paid to British farmers for most kinds of produce, for instance, are fixed by the Ministry of Agriculture after an annual review, and the prices at which most branded goods, from breakfast cereals to motor cars, are sold in British shops are fixed (no doubt after very careful examination of the market) by the manufacturers. Some prices, again, are fixed deliberately, but only after a process of negotiation. Of these, the prices of the various kinds of labour—wage and salary rates—provide the clearest example. Yet others are, in a sense, not 'fixed' at all—nobody makes a deliberate decision which he regards as determining the price in question; it emerges in the market as the result of decisions by a great many people, each of whom probably thinks that he is 'following the market' rather than influencing it. This is true of the prices in the 'free world markets' for many of the main foodstuffs and raw materials.

There are some other mechanisms by which prices are immediately determined and many sub-species of the mechanisms which we have just listed; but it will suffice for our purpose if we look at three kinds of mechanism—the free market, the fixing of prices for branded manufactured goods, and the determination of wage and salary rates.

The Free Markets

Nearly all the main raw materials and foodstuffs which are traded internationally have, at some time, been sold in markets which were completely 'free' in the sense that no governments or associations of producers attempted to control prices in them or the quantities of product placed upon them. Many of them still are free in this sense. Australian wool, for instance is produced year by year in quantities which are the result of decisions about sheep-rearing taken some years before, and of the weather and the

60

incidence of diseases and parasites in the meantime. Each year's clip is sold by the growers—they hardly ever hold any appreciable amount back—in competition with wool from elsewhere. It is bought by a great number of merchants and processors at a price—or rather, a great many prices corresponding to the very many kinds and grades of wool. How is the general level of these prices, ruling at any one time, determined?

It seems realistic to say that it is determined, immediately, by three things—the orders which the merchants and processors already have or anticipate from their customers for wool or wool products, how much wool they already have, and the state of their expectations about the future movements of prices. The bigger the orders they have on hand, or expect, the more urgent their need for wool becomes, the more they are willing to pay to get more, and the more they will have to be paid for parting with any. In general, size of orders depends largely on the size of the customers' incomes; if they can afford more, they buy more. Prices of many things therefore, are sensitive to income in the communities which use them. Shortage of stocks on hand will have the same kind of effect on the prices the buyers are willing to pay, or that they will demand for wool sold, as abundance of orders from their customers. This is simply a version of the famous interaction of supply and demand—supply in the sense of stocks on hand and demand in the sense of current or anticipated drain from them. But the third factor—expectations about prices—can be just as important. Unless they are in a great hurry, buyers will not pay a particular price for wool if they expect the price soon to be appreciably lower. In the same way, it is clear that sellers will not usually take a particular price if they expect they would, by waiting a moderate time, get appreciably more. Any widespread increase in the prices that people in the market expect to rule in future is therefore bound to raise prices at once, and and widespread fall in expected future prices to lower them.

The question then becomes, why people should expect the future level of prices to be different from the level in the recent past. One very good reason for doing so arises when there is any news suggesting that the rate of production of wool (or whatever commodity is under discussion) is going to be different from what it has been—or rather, different from what it has hitherto been expected to be. It is clear that, provided the level of the ultimate buyers' incomes, and their preference for things which embody the commodity in question do not change, it will be possible to get them to take up an increased annual supply of it only by lowering its price. Or, to look at the matter in another way, if the rate of supply increases to a level above the rate of use, stocks will accumulate, and this, by itself, will make people in the market less willing to buy more and more willing to get rid of some. An increased annual supply must therefore mean that price will be lower than hitherto—or, at any rate, lower on the average over any considerable period of time. In the same way, news that leads the market to expect a higher rate of consumption or use of the commodity (without any corresponding change in the conditions under which it is produced) creates a legitimate expectation that price will over some future period be higher, on the average, than it has recently been. And such expectations, as we have seen, will move price at once to something near its expected level.

It might seem, therefore, that the price ruling in a market at any moment is a sort of average of the prices expected by all the dealers in it, and that these expectations relate to what economists call the 'long-period equilibrium price'—that is to say, the average price which would have to rule over a considerable period (perhaps a number of years) in order that the amount of the commodity produced in that period and the amount taken up for final consumption or use should be about equal. It might also be felt that, since the dealers in question are the people with the strongest incentive and the best opportunity to estimate the long period equilibrium price, such an average of their views will not be very far wrong. If this were true, then free market prices would be reasonably steady; whenever a rise in supply or a fall in ultimate demand for a commodity was (correctly) foreseen, the price would fall smoothly so as to reach the new equilibrium level just as the anticipated rise or fall became effective, and anticipated reductions in supply or increases in final demand would raise price in the same orderly way.

In fact, free market prices are notoriously variable. For many commodities the highest price recorded in most years is more than a third as big again as the lowest price recorded in the same year; for several of them the annual average price has rarely or never varied over less than a two-fold range within any period of five years, and has sometimes increased or decreased three- or four-fold. If prices which do this are formed in the way we have suggested, it seems that the markets must be remarkably bad at interpreting the indications they receive with regard to the probable future changes in production and consumption. It does, indeed, seem on closer inspection that some markets greatly overrate the importance of the information they receive. Their reactions to news of reduced production of the commodity—a poor crop, for instance—seems often to be such as would be justified only on the assumption that consumption has to be reduced correspondingly. This is very rarely a justifiable assumption—the markets for most agricultural products which suffer from year-to-year variations in growing conditions contains a reserve or 'carry-over' of the commodity which is several times as large as the amount by which one year's crop is likely to fall below normal. All that a small crop need mean, as a rule, therefore, is that stocks will be drawn upon and will remain below normal until there is a big crop.

Why do markets exaggerate the significance of temporary changes in the outlook in this way? Probably the main reason is that the people in them are not all, as we suggested earlier, trying to guess the long-term equilibrium price. Most of them are not really interested in the average price likely to rule over (say) the next five years; they are concerned with what price is likely to be a few weeks or months hence, when they expect next to have to buy or sell. This means that they are interested primarily in what the rest of the market is going to think at that time. If enough people believe that most other people in the market will make a drastic adjustment of the price they are willing to offer or take, in response to some piece of news of purely temporary significance about the supply or consumption of the commodity, this belief will be justified by a drastic change in price. It becomes irrelevant, for their purpose, to ask whether the news really justifies a big change in the estimate of probable average price over the next five years—and probably they do not ask themselves this question.

So much for the day-to-day or (in some markets) year-to-year variations in price, which may be attributed mainly to the excessive notice which markets are apt to take of ephemeral changes in outlook. Over a longer period, as we have already hinted, the general, or average level of price in a market is bound to be close to the long-term equilibrium price; it is bound to be such as will induce people to produce and to consume nearly equal amounts of the commodity. Production can exceed or fall below consumption by a large percentage for a month, and by a considerable percentage for a year, but not for a decade—the storage-capacity, the amount of stocks which is ever in existence, and the amounts which people are willing to hold are, for most commodities, only a small proportion of ten years' production or consumption.

But the establishment of the long-run equilibrium price is impeded by more than the excessive sensitiveness of the market's response to news—in many cases it is made difficult because producers respond excessively to changes in price. This trouble was first analysed by economists in the particular instance of changes in the supply and price of pigs, and the 'pig cycle' has accordingly come to be referred to as typical of fluctuations of this sort. In fact, similar troubles arise wherever producers vary their planned output sufficiently according as the price of their product is high or low, so long as it is also the case that it takes a considerable time for their plans to mature, and for the increased or decreased rate of production they decide upon to reach the market. If prices are high, for instance, they may plan to increase production; but because the increased production does not eventuate for some time, price in the meantime stays high, perhaps giving them confidence to extend their plans still more. Eventually, the increased output reaches the market, stocks rise, and prices fall. Production plans are then reduced, and after a time the flow of product reaching the market will decrease, so that stocks are worked off and prices rise again. Of course, if dealers in the market knew of the increased or decreased production plans soon enough, and responded by expecting (and thus bringing about) lower or higher prices at once, this would choke off the excessive adjustments of the producers and stabilize price. To some extent this no doubt happens; if it did not, price and output fluctuations of the 'pig-cycle' variety would be much more drastic than they are. But they are quite sufficiently troublesome as it is, not only in many kinds of agriculture, but also in some branches of manufacture such as shipbuilding, where the product takes a long time to design and finish.

We may sum up and conclude this sketch of the working of free markets as follows. Over any long period such as five or ten years, the amount of a commodity which is produced will, in most cases depend on the average level of its price, being greater if price is higher. The amount of it which is consumed or put to use by its final buyers will also depend on the average price, being generally lower if price is higher. And, in such a long period, the average level of price must be such as to make the quantity produced and the quantity consumed not very different from each other. This determination of the level of price by the condition that supply and demand must be nearly equal can equally well be described as the equalization of supply and demand (in the sense of total production and total consumption over a long period) by the price mechanism. It has great virtues—it spreads the impact of increases and decreases in supply over all the consumers in a way which has some relation to their willingness to take more or less of the good, and it causes increases and decreases in demand to be transmitted back to all the sources of supply, and to affect their respective outputs in a way which bears some relation to their efficiencies.

But it also has troubles. Supply and price may tend to fluctuate not only because of natural variations in production, but because of delayed responses of supply to price changes. And even in short periods during which rate of production does not change appreciably, price may jump up and down irregularly because of excessive or arbitrary reactions of the people in the market to news which has some relation to future supply and consumption, or which is thought to affect the expectations of other people in the market.

Control Schemes
These imperfections in the working of free markets are among the reasons why a good many of them have ceased to be free—that is to say, have come under some kind of central regulation. Fluctuations in supply which are generated by the working of the market mechanism, and are not directly in line with variations in demand, are clearly disturbing; they cause variation in the incomes of producers of the commodity concerned, and the fortunes of users of it alike. The same is true of the short-term variations in price, not closely related to changes in supply, which introduce an element of uncertainty into the affairs of all who deal in the commodity at all. But attempts to regulate previously free markets have perhaps as often been inspired by the desire to escape a process of permanent adjustment to changes in demand, or to changes in the source of supply, and they have in some cases turned into schemes for exploiting the market in the interests of producers by restricting the total supply, and so keeping the price well above the long-term equilibrium level which should have been aimed at if the purpose had been simply price stabilization. In many cases this has been done by either government or private action, not in the world market as a whole, but within one country which was sufficiently insulated against imports by tariffs or other restrictions to make it possible for it to maintain an internal price for the product in question which was substantially higher than the price elsewhere. But it has also been done on a world-wide scale in certain cases.

Where all, or nearly all of the world supply of a commodity comes from a single country, it is particularly easy to regulate production, exports, or prices of it in such a way as to bring extra profits to the producers, or to the producing country. This happened with Sicilian sulphur, German potash, Chilean iodine, and Japanese camphor in the nineteenth century. Before the first world

E

war, it had happened to a number of other commodities in which the number of producers, or the producing area, was small—diamonds, nickel, aluminium, and quinine. The end of that war left enormous tasks of readjustment in the markets for a number of commodities, where supply had been stimulated by war-time conditions and abnormal stocks accumulated—sugar, copper, and wool, for instance. In some cases (e.g. wool) governments intervened to hold surplus stocks and sell them off gradually; in others, as the great fluctuations of income of the post-war years imposed still further burdens on the market mechanism, producers or governments began to take steps to reduce production where surpluses existed. These control schemes of the nineteen-twenties were largely ill-conceived. The two most famous and disastrous examples were the British rubber restriction scheme and the Brazilian coffee scheme. In both cases, part of the reason for failure was that the restriction of production (or sales) was not sufficiently comprehensive; the restriction which those operating the two schemes imposed upon themselves raised prices also for non-members, who, in the longer run, would simply have increased their proportions of world output, at the expense of the members. There were other troubles, too—the Brazilians could not get enough credit to enable them to store the surplus coffee from two bumper harvests, while the rubber scheme incurred the odium of having contributed to a spectacular price-boom when demand suddenly rose after a period of restricted production. In any case, however, the great fall in world demand with the slump of the early thirties both over-burdened the majority of the restriction schemes which had hitherto been set up and, at the same time provided a new incentive for restriction.

The nineteen-thirties were, accordingly, a period of renewed and extended attempts to keep supply of foodstuffs and raw materials in line with demand by restriction of production or marketing, and at the same time, in most cases, to keep the general levels of price favourable to the producers. Sugar, wheat, tin, lead, oil, steel, rubber, zinc, and copper were all brought under some measure of fairly comprehensive control, at least for a time. Experience was gained of both the possible benefits and the difficulties of regulation of this kind, and in the general discussion of economic policy which subsequently took place during and after the second world war, much attention was given to the possibility of providing stability in world markets without either exploiting the consumer or preventing the replacement of old sources of supply by cheaper new ones.

As a result of this, fairly widespread approval grew up for methods of marketing which gave the importers as well as the exporters of the products in question a voice in deciding what should be done, and which allowed a good deal of flexibility. Unlike the period after the first world war, however, the period since the second has not favoured the growth of control schemes. The great surplus of wool in existence at the end of the war was again marketed by an inter-governmental organization, which disposed of it all by 1950; in most of the commodity markets, however, there were shortages rather than surpluses in the post-war decade, and producers therefore had little incentive to combine for the regulation of amounts produced or marketed. Importing countries do not seem yet to have appreciated the advantages which they might gain from joining in control schemes which might protect them against price booms, such as that which followed the outbreak of the Korean war in 1950.

The present position, therefore, is that wheat, sugar, and tin are the subjects of what may be called 'new-style' agreements involving importing countries as well as exporters, and that, of the major international agreements between producers made before the war, only that relating to tea has been continuously renewed. The wheat, sugar, and tin agreements each embody a 'floor' and a 'ceiling' price, between which it is, in part, the object of the scheme to keep the actual market price of the commodity in question. In the wheat scheme, the producing countries undertake to supply to other members, and the importing countries to take from them, certain definite annual quantities of wheat annually, at prices within the prescribed range, during the period to which the agreement applies, though, so long as these obligations are fulfilled, other transactions are permitted without restriction. (In fact, the United Kingdom refused to adhere to the agreement from 1953 onwards hoping that it would be able to buy wheat below the 'floor' price then fixed.)

The sugar agreement fixes the maximum amounts which exporting countries are allowed to sell in the free market (i.e. apart from certain regional transactions to which the agreement does not apply), and calls upon them so to control their production that their stocks vary only within prescribed limits. The importing countries agree simply to refrain from increasing their purchases from countries outside the agreement above the level at which they stood before it came into effect—thus giving the exporters some assurance that there will be a continued demand for their sugar.

The tin agreement is the most elaborate of the three. The Council which administers it not only fixes the amounts of tin which producing countries are allowed to export, the total permitted exports being adjusted so as to meet the expected demand at a price within the prescribed range, but it actually holds money and stocks of tin—'buffer stocks'—with which it operates in the tin market to correct any departure of the price outside that range. Perhaps this comes nearest to being the model to which control schemes will have to conform if they are to have power to adjust supply to demand in an orderly way, and to eliminate the short-term fluctuations in price which are due to changes in the markets' expectations.

Apart from these instances of inter-governmental control designed to regulate world prices, there are some other cases in which the policy of a government is instrumental in greatly influencing the world price of a commodity. The most important of these is oil. Here, the key factor is the level of production in the United States, which is controlled by a number of public authorities there on the general ground that unregulated oil production would lead to a scramble for the limited quantity known to exist in the earth at any one time. Such a scramble has been known to produce such a glut of oil in the market that the price was driven down far too low to cover the cost of drilling and, still more, the cost of prospecting for new oil deposits. American output regulation is designed, therefore, to enable these costs to be covered in American conditions. Partly because a large part of oil production in the rest of the world is carried on by American companies, and partly for reasons which can now be described as historical, the price charged for Middle Eastern and some other oil is geared to that of oil in the United States, so that production policy there governs the price for most of the world.

The United States Government's policy of 'supporting' the prices of American farm products also plays an important part in influencing world prices of those products, in so far as it tends to encourage production of them, and to lead to surpluses which are afterwards sold in the world market—generally at a loss to the government. On the other hand, this tendency to produce surpluses has been offset from time to time by paying farmers to limit their production. The West African countries have, on the other hand, probably influenced the supply of cocoa in a downward direction, on the whole, by paying farmers less than the world price. The silk market is much more strongly influenced by the policy of the Japanese government in operating a control scheme of its own, complete with floor and ceiling prices and buffer stocks—since Japan is responsible for four-fifths of world silk exports.

Instances of this kind could be greatly multiplied. There are few commodities which are not subject to governmental price-fixing or output regulation, or encouragement, in some part of the world. On the other hand, those quantities of most foodstuffs and raw materials which enter into international trade are still sold in more or less free markets, where the average levels of their prices over long periods are determined by the condition that they should be such as, along with the numerous other factors at work, will make the average rates of production and use nearly equal, and where short period variations in production, use, and expectations create severe fluctuations in price from month to month or year to year. It is in this that food stuffs and raw materials differ most from manufactured products.

Manufactured Goods

The typical manufactured product—a particular model of motor car, a cloth of a particular design, a soap powder, or a novel—is different in some way from all others, and is probably made by advertisement to appear still more so to prospective purchasers. This means that the manufacturer can decide on the price at which he will sell; he is not in the position of the farmer, producing wheat of the same grade as that grown by thousands of other farmers, who will find that there is a market price for that wheat, above which he cannot sell, and below which he would be foolish to sell. If the manufacturer sells at somewhat above the price charged by his competitors for the most nearly comparable products (claiming, of course, that his product is better than theirs), he will still sell some, because some people will believe his claim of superior quality—may, indeed, find that his product suits their peculiar needs better than others. If he sells at a rather lower price, his sales will probably be larger. There is no single price which is imposed upon him by the conditions of the market; he is free to choose which price out of a considerable range will do best for him.

If the manufacturer knew how much his sales would rise in response to a particular price-reduction, he could choose the price which would bring him the greatest profit. A large body of economic theory has grown upon the assumption that this is what manufacturers (in fact, sellers generally) may be expected to do. But, in practice, manufacturers never know with any considerable precision how price and volume of sales are related to one another. In some instances, however, they seek, by trial and error, or by 'hunch', for the price which will make their profits as big as possible—a price which will, of course, be higher when demand is strong (when buyers' incomes are high, for instance), and lower when it is weak. This is, essentially, the policy of 'charging what the market will bear'. It is perhaps most likely to be found in operation where the seller has the greatest difficulty in knowing the cost of producing and selling the particular kind of product in question (still more in deciding the cost of any single unit of output), because the costs of that and other units and kinds of production are too inextricably mixed up together. In such a situation, all he can do is make a guess at the most remunerative price, and hope that what he gets in this way from all the goods he sells, together, will more than cover his total costs, leaving him with a profit of some kind. The prices of gas, electricity, and (though here we step outside manufacturing industry), the rates charged by railways are traditionally among the most strongly determined by estimates of what the market will bear.

On the other hand, there are many situations in which this consideration takes second place, and the manufacturer's chief attention in choosing the prices of his products is given to their cost. Naturally, this is most likely to happen when the costs that are attributable to the production of the particular good in question are most easily identifiable. This will be the case in industries like tailoring, for instance, where most of the costs of production are direct costs of labour and materials embodied in particular units of output—not 'overhead' costs which the manufacturer has to incur to stay in business at all, whether he produces a particular piece of output or not. But there are other considerations which make many manufacturers look at costs rather than at the state of the market. One is the impossibility, which may sometimes exist, of even guessing the response of sales to a change in price, especially where it is not very practicable to experiment by changing price frequently. This impossibility of guessing confidently how sales depend on price may arise in many cases from the probability that the firm's competitors (or some of them) would respond to any price-change by altering their prices also, coupled with uncertainty as to just how they would alter them.

An interesting—and probably a rather common—variant of this situation is that where each of a number of competing manufacturers is inclined to take a cautious or pessimistic view of the probable effects of any change he may introduce in his own prices— he thinks that if he raises them, his competitors will keep theirs down and steal a good many of his customers, while if he lowers them, they will follow him, so that he will not gain much trade. If all think like this, there will be a tendency for them not to change their prices without very good cause. Since, however, costs change, and most such changes (e.g. changes in the prices of raw materials, or in wage-rates) presumably affect all firms producing rather similar products in much the same way, each firm may feel some confidence that, if it alters its prices only to keep them in line with costs, it will keep in line also with its competitors. Once it comes to be thought that other firms probably adjust their prices in some sort of relation to their costs, this becomes the safe thing for each firm to do.

Where the products sold (or the processes carried out) by the different manufacturers are very similar, a situation of this kind can still arise, provided that the number of competing firms is not very great, or, at any rate, that there are some firms which are so big in relation to the whole industry that they have to reckon on changes in their price policy being noted, and perhaps imitated by a substantial part of their competitors. In fact, in the United Kingdom, at least, it very often happens that firms in industries of this kind take formal steps to achieve common prices, based upon cost. This is usually done through a trade association to which the firms in question belong; in many instances members submit their costs for producing the various products to the federation, which subsequently advises them on the prices to be adopted—prices generally based upon some kind of average of the members' costs. Such practices would be contrary to the law in the United States and Canada, but, where they occur, they clearly establish a strong connection between the costs of producing goods (in the industry as a whole) and the prices at which they are sold.

The distinction we have made between industries where prices are consciously related to estimates of what the market will bear, and industries where they are consciously related to costs probably exaggerates the difference which emerges in practice between the results in the two kinds of case. Where prices are fixed primarily with an eye on the market, the condition of the market itself often varies in a way which tends to make prices, in fact, move with costs. If some circumstance enables an industry to make increased profits, competition both from new firms coming in and from existing firms expanding is likely to check the increase, or after a time to reverse it. If profits on a line of goods fall, there will be a tendency for some firms to cease or to cut down their production of that particular line, thus eventually restoring the fortunes of the firms which still sell it.

Similarly, where prices are fixed predominantly by adding a 'mark-up' to direct costs of production, the circumstances of the market are still liable to have some effect on the size of the mark-up. At times when trade unions are pressing strongly for higher wages and employers are not optimistic about their ability to sell their products at higher prices, for instance, the profit margin may get squeezed.

On the whole, when one looks at the way in which what the price that the buyer pays for manufactured goods in the United Kingdom, at least, is divided between the profits and the costs of the various manufacturers and distributors taken all together, one is struck by the constancy of the ratio between the two. It is true that, in depressions when incomes and sales are low, the ratio of profits to costs is also low because some costs, such as salaries and rent, do not go down with sales, even if wage and raw materials' costs do. There is also some evidence that between the two world wars the conventional mark-ups in the United Kingdom were lower than before 1914, and that they may have risen a little since the second world war. They are, of course, very different in different industries. It seems, however, to be broadly true, probably in all the chief manufacturing countries, that the prices of manufactures are mainly determined, directly or indirectly, by cost, in the sense that the average rate of profit—the margin between cost and price—varies relatively little. Certainly this marks them off sharply from most foodstuffs and raw materials, the prices of which, determined in mainly free markets, do not vary at all closely with anything which could be called average cost of production—a quantity which would in many cases be exceedingly difficult to determine. The same is true also of some other important kinds of price—the rates and fares charged in liner shipping and in air transport—which are fixed by international agreements between companies. The evidence is that these, too, vary rather closely with costs.

The Price of Labour

The costs of production of manufactured goods, and, indeed, of the 'services' which also enter largely into the output of any advanced economy, consist to a great extent of costs of labour. Of the value of goods and services sold by firms in the United Kingdom each year, whether for home consumption or for export, something over half consists of wages and salaries, about a sixth of costs of imported materials, rather under a twentieth of rent. A good deal of the remaining 35 per cent.—perhaps a third of it—consists of fixed interest payments which producers must make; the rest is 'profit' in the rather loose sense that it is earned by people either on the capital they have invested in businesses, or by running their own businesses, but is not fixed in advance by any contractual arrangement, as interest, rent, wages, and salaries are.

We need not trouble here about the way in which rent and interest are fixed, but may concentrate upon the big items—wages and salaries. We shall return later to some discussion of the factors which determine differences between individual incomes from these sources; we are concerned now rather with what determines the aggregate levels.

There are very considerable differences between countries in the mechanisms at work. Overwhelmingly in the United Kingdom and to a not very much smaller extent on the United States and the industrial countries of western continental Europe, wages (and important classes of salaries) are fixed by collective bargaining, between a trade union and an employers' organization, or perhaps between a trade union and a firm. Even where this mechanism operates, the actual wages paid may be above the agreed rates, to an extent which depends upon the strength with which employers in a particulary industry, or in a particular district, compete against each other for labour. In some occupations there is no or little union organization, and wages are either determined by something approaching a free market mechanism or are fixed (at least as to the minimum amounts which may be paid) by the state or some tribunal appointed by it. On the whole, however, it is correct to regard collective bargaining between trade unions and employers' organizations as the typical method of wage determination in western industrial countries. It is also true to say that the way this bargaining goes is the most important of the *immediate* causes affecting the general levels of prices in such countries—or, at any rate, affecting the prices of manufactured goods and of services.

How, then, does collective bargaining work? For a long time now in most of the countries concerned the initiative in operating it has come mainly from the trade unions in the form of requests for wage-increases or the equivalent (that is to say, shortening of the working week, paid holidays, or some other improvement in conditions of employment). Employers' organizations, naturally, rather rarely take the initiative in proposing wage increases, and proposals also for decreases have been rare at most times—and virtually unheard of in the past generation.

Demands for wage-increases depend, of course, on a great many things, including the general political situation in the country, the attitude of the government, and the strength and militancy of trade union leadership, but the main economic factors which tend to be quoted to substantiate claims, and which probably play leading parts in creating them are rises in the cost of living, wage-increases (or sometimes increases in earnings due to more overtime work) secured by workers in other industries, and the feeling, based upon views either about profits or about price-policy in the industry immediately concerned, that it can afford to pay higher wages.

Probably the order in which these have been stated is their usual order of importance; rises in the cost of living come first. Sometimes the adjustment is automatic or nearly so; French wages have lately tended to vary closely with an official minimum wage calculated from cost of living data; the Australian minimum wages were for a long time similarly calculated; a substantial number of wage and salary earners in the United Kingdom have a cost of living clause in their agreements with their employers, and up to a fifth of the wage increases in some recent years have been due to the operation of such 'sliding scales'. But even where the adjustment for rising cost of living is not automatic it tends to be claimed by trade unions, though there is often a considerable delay in this, especially if the cost of living is rising only slowly—when its rate of increase is really noticeable claims for wage-increase based upon it tend to be more prompt and frequent. Where the final wage award depends on an arbitration tribunal or some other independent body, claims based upon cost of living appear to carry great weight.

Great weight is also carried, however, both with impartial wage-awarding bodies and with the unions themselves, by what has happened to wages in other industries. The 'differentials' between one group of workers and another (footplate men and other railway workers, London and provincial bus drivers, and to a smaller extent operatives in different industries) are very jealously guarded; they are badges of status as well as parts of money income. It is very difficult to raise the wage or salary rates of any substantial group without increasing the probability that some other groups will demand, and will get, increases also. A period in which some kinds of labour are becoming scarcer, relatively to the demand for them, than others therefore tends to be one of general wage-increase; the market mechanism tends to raise the wages of the scarcer kinds, and those of at least some of the others tend to move up in sympathy, even though there may at the time be a surplus of labour in relation to the demand for it in some of these other cases. This has been a powerful source of wage-increase in the United Kingdom and some other European countries since the war, with particular kinds of labour (e.g. coal-miners) very scarce. The fact that there has been full employment has very greatly helped this tendency, since in these conditions employers are anxious to maintain the wage rates of their employees relatively to those paid in other industries—they are willing to go some way in raising wages to prevent their labour supply from being diverted to firms where there have been increases already.

It is not possible to be so definite about the effect of profits on wage-increases. High profits are sometimes given as reasons for demanding higher wages, and it is certainly true that higher wages are more likely to be conceded if there are already high profits. This no doubt helps to explain why, as we have seen, profits do not vary greatly as a proportion of total income.

The General Level of Prices

We have now glanced at the main ways in which the price-determining mechanisms seem to work in western countries. For the most part, the prices of raw materials (especially such as enter into international trade) are formed in the free market by supply and demand; they fluctuate widely, and are particularly sensitive to changes in income and in expectations. The prices of manufactured goods are, no doubt, sensitive in some degree directly to changes in income, and perhaps in expectations too, but mainly they are based upon cost of production, with a profit margin which does not really vary very much from time to time. The prices of the various kinds of labour, also, are in some degree sensitive to immediate supply and demand changes; a great shortage of labour in a particular industry will cause employers to bid against each other, for instance; but in the main they are fixed for considerable periods by collective bargaining, and depend largely upon the cost of living and movements in the prices of other kinds of labour, and partly upon the level of profits and the general level of economic activity and employment.

The prices of finished goods and services are compounded, therefore, mainly of the prices of labour and raw materials, and since they are the elements of which the cost of living is composed, they help in turn to determine wages and salaries. This interdependence can make any change ricochet through the economy; a rise in raw material prices for instance, not only makes for a (proportionately smaller) direct increase in the prices of finished goods, but since this in turn raises the cost of living, it will lead to demands (usually partially successful) for higher wages, which raise costs of finished goods, and so the cost of living, still more. The resulting series of increases usually seems to die away somewhat before the cost of living has been raised in the same proportion as the initial increases in raw material prices; in any case, it is rather a slow-moving series, and since the sharper movements in raw material prices are in many cases quickly reversed, the prices of finished goods often have not time to respond to them very much before receiving an opposite impulse, and consequently follow a comparatively sedate course.

It is only when prices of primary products move for a long time in one direction (as between 1939 and 1951, for instance) that they have a great power of dragging all other prices with them, and even then how far they do so depends on a great many highly variable factors. A persistent movement of primary product prices can, however, combine with the resulting movement of prices of manufactures to produce a powerful effect; a rise in primary product prices, for instance, can cause a series of upward movements in industrial wages, salaries, and prices which involve increases in the total money incomes of industrial communities. These mean that there is more money to spend on primary products, which therefore rise in price again, and the whole process repeats itself. Something like this has probably been going on in the world since 1939, and especially since 1945.

In all this discussion of prices we have not yet mentioned the influence of monetary policy—that is to say, of the terms on which monetary authorities are willing to supply money in response to demand for it, or of their more positive action in pushing more of it into circulation on their own initiative, or, on the other hand, removing some from circulation. This is a large subject, of which we can only take note here in passing. It is obvious that if the authorities bring about a shortage of money, they will tend to lower those prices which are sensitive to the general state of demand and supply. People who want to lay in stocks of raw materials, for instance, will find that they cannot get the money to buy them; people who have stocks of raw materials and want to buy other things (new machinery, for example), will have no means of getting the money for their purchases except selling some of their raw material stocks. The reduced inquiries for materials to buy and the increased offers for sale will depress prices, and once dealers in the markets realize that the authorities are, in fact, pursuing a restrictive monetary policy with some determination, expectations of lower price will arise, and produce their usual effect of bringing about the event anticipated. It must be borne in mind, however, that most of the primary product markets are in some sense world markets; prices move together in all the countries which trade fairly freely with each other in the commodities concerned, and it is the total situation in all these markets together which determines prices. A restrictive monetary policy in one country therefore, will not produce much effect on world prices, unless that country contains a high proportion of all the purchasing power normally directed to buying the commodities in question.

When we come to wages and salaries, or to prices of finished products the effect of monetary policy is much less direct. If a change in monetary policy is sufficiently widespread to alter primary product prices, that, of course, will influence cost of production of manufactures directly, and, since (after a time) it will influence cost of living, it is likely to have some effect upon demands for higher wages—it will speed them up if it is expansionary, and slow them down if it is contractionary. This, in turn, will work upon costs of production, and then upon wages and salaries again in the way we have discussed.

There is another indirect effect. Monetary policy raises or lowers the ability of both consumers and firms to buy manufactured goods. The direct effect of this on their prices is relatively small, because, as we have seen, those prices depend mainly upon costs. In the same way, its direct effect upon the price of labour is relatively small, because wages and salaries are not mainly fixed by competition between employers to get labour. But if the ability to buy manufactured goods is reduced, stocks will pile up, orders will be cut down, and there will be both a reduction in employment and a reduced demand for materials. The reduced demand for materials will certainly reinforce and prolong the more immediate effect which we have noted of a restrictive policy in depressing the prices of raw materials, with all the further consequences of that upon other prices. But will an increase of unemployment affect the price of labour?

To some extent it may be expected to work in that direction. When there is substantial unemployment, profits are normally low and the prospect of increasing them by raising prices remote. Employers, therefore, are generally resistant to wage increases in these conditions. There is some tendency, too, for trade unions to be less militant when many of their members are out of work, and there are not high profits to tantalize them. Often, periods of unemployment are also periods of general world-wide depression when prices of primary products, and so the cost of living, are falling, and this circumstance certainly restrains claims for higher wages. But the evidence is that the existence of unemployment alone, not accompanied by steady or falling cost of living, is not a very powerful reducer of wage-demands—or even of wage increases—in most modern economies. A generation or two ago, when labour was less strongly organized in most countries than it is now, and wages depended more upon competition between employers, it was somewhat more effective, but it seems that we must now reckon on rather a high rate of unemployment being required to produce a moderate reduction in the rate of wage-increase. This limits the effectiveness of monetary stringency as a restraint on general price-increase, or as a promoter of general price-decrease; but it does not mean that it has no effectiveness at all. As we have seen, monetary policy can make a good deal of difference to the course of prices by its immediate impact on the primary product markets—provided that it is sufficiently widely pursued—and it is also true, of course, that it can have drastic and far-reaching effects, acting partly through the level of employment, if society is willing to tolerate wide variations in employment for that purpose.

The Terms of Trade

While the general level of prices is important, and the discussion of it follows naturally from our consideration of the ways in which prices are formed, it is now time to remind ourselves that how good a living family or an economy get will normally depend rather upon *relative* prices. How much of the things it wants can be got in return for a unit of the things it produces can be measured by taking the ratio of the price-level of its exports to the price-level of its imports. This ratio—or sometimes the inverse of it, which measures how much of the things it produces must be given up in exchange for a unit of the things it wants—is known as the community's 'terms of trade'. The less self-sufficient the community is, the more important are its terms of trade in determining, along with its productiveness, how good a living it gets.

Let us consider a community which exports a single primary commodity, such as wool. Our consideration of primary commodity prices in the free market has shown that the average price of wool over (say) any decade must be such as to make the total production of wool and the total use of wool over that decade nearly equal; it will be lower if circumstances increase the output of wool which is grown in response to any given price, and it will be higher if circumstances increase the amount of wool which the world wants to use at any given price. How much wool the world uses at any given price of wool depends on many things, including fashions in clothing and the prices of other textile fibres which can be used instead of wool; but most of all it depends on world income—the money value of all the world's output.

The same is true of the things which the wool-exporting community imports; their average prices in any decade will be related to the amounts of them produced and the total world income (though of course changes in tastes and the rise of substitutes also complicate the picture). As a first approximation, therefore, we might say that, since world income affects the prices both of wool and of the things imported in exchange for it, in such a way that a rise in income raises both of them, these two effects will cancel out. This would leave us with the respective world outputs of wool and of the things the wool-producers buy as the sole factors affecting their terms of trade. A country's terms of trade will depend, roughly, on the ratio of the world output of the things it exports to the world output of the things it imports. If that ratio rises, the country's terms of trade are likely to deteriorate; it will have to give more exports for a unit of imports. A community which exported wool and imported, say, tropical products might well pray for heavy crops in the tropics, poor wool production by the rest of the world, and (unless it is already responsible for a large proportion of world wool production), a large wool output of its own.

But this is, indeed, only a first approximation, and a very crude one at that. We cannot really leave world income out of the reckoning, because the prices of a country's imports and of its exports will usually be sensitive to it in different degrees. As income rises (or, at least, as real income per head rises), there is, as we shall see in Chapter 8, a tendency to spend higher proportions of income on manufactures, and lower proportions on primary commodities (especially foodstuffs). A calculation by Professor Lewis implies that, with world income expanding as it did in the fifty years before 1929, the world tended to increase its consumption of manufactured goods at 4 per cent. per annum, but its consumption of foodstuffs at only 2 per cent. per annum. If outputs of the two classes of goods had increased at the same rate, therefore—if the ratio between their outputs had stayed constant—a relative glut of foodstuffs would have developed, and the terms of trade of food-exporting communities would have deteriorated.

We can look at this in another way. If real income increases, there is an increased demand for most kinds of goods. As we have noted, the increase in demand for manufactures will generally be greater, proportionately, than the increase in demand for foodstuffs, but both these increases will call forth increased supplies—we are thinking here of what happens over a period of years, in which supply has time to adjust itself to demand. To call forth an increased supply of foodstuffs, it will generally be necessary to raise their prices more than the price of manufactures would have to be raised if a similar expansion in their output was needed.

To get more foodstuffs, it is usually necessary to use land that was too unprofitable to use before, or else to get more out of land already in use at an increased cost per unit, while facilities for manufacturing can usually be expanded without much increase in costs of processing—often, indeed with a reduction of costs made possible by the larger scale of working. It follows, therefore, that if the world was determined to expand its supplies of foodstuffs and of manufacturers in the same proportion, it would have to raise the price of foodstuffs in relation to that of manufacturers in order to do so. In fact, as we have noted, the effect of higher incomes is to make the world increase its demand for manufactures faster, proportionately, than its demand for foodstuffs, so that we cannot say there is any general presumption that costs per unit of output will rise in food production in relation to what they are in manufacturing. What happens to the terms of trade of food-exporting communities, or to their inverse, the terms of trade of manufacturing communities which import food, as total demand rises, depends on the precise balance between two things—the shift in demand towards manufactures and the way in which the relative costs of production of two kinds of goods vary with the quantities in which they are produced.

While we might hope to be able to say something about the way in which an expansion of world income would affect these terms of trade over the next few years, assuming that such things as technical knowledge and the political and social obstacles to its full application remain in the present state, we have to admit that the changes which both the technology and the obstacles undergo in the course of time are unpredictable, and are really the major factors affecting the terms of trade. The application of enormous improvements in manufacturing, especially of iron, steel, and textiles, between about 1750 and 1850 very greatly cheapened manufactures in relation to foodstuffs, and worsened the terms of trade of manufacturing communities—though since their outputs of manufactures per hour of their labour increased to a still greater extent, the amounts of imported foodstuffs which they could buy with the products of an hour's labour actually increased. After that, and especially after about 1870, the effect of transport improvements in opening up new overseas areas as foodstuff exporters, plus general improvements in agricultural methods, enabled foodstuffs to get cheaper in relation to manufactures, in spite of the constantly more rapid growth of demand for the latter. This trend seems to have come to an end before the second world war, but it is plain that, since we cannot predict either inventions or the speed of their application, we cannot say whether, on a longer view, it has really come to an end or not.

In the shorter run, however, changes in terms of trade are a good deal more predictable. Over a few months or even up to four or five years, as we have noted, prices of manufactures are steady in comparison with those of foodstuffs and raw materials, partly because of the different mechanisms by which the two sets of prices are determined, partly because output of manufactured goods is quicker to respond to changes—particularly to falls—in demand for them than is output of many raw materials and foodstuffs, especially those of agricultural origin. It follows from this that, in a boom when incomes and activity rise at more than the average rate at which they grow in the longer run, the terms of trade generally turn in favour of the primary producing countries, whereas when the growth of world income is checked or turns for the time into a decline, the terms of trade go the other way. It is as well to remember, however, that, while demands for the different raw materials and foodstuffs change to a large extent in parallel with each other—changes in world income being responsible for this parallelism—their conditions of supply are strongly influenced by mineral discoveries, local rainfall, diseases and other irregular occurrences which mostly affect them one at a time. The prices of the different raw materials and foodstuffs therefore follow very considerably different courses from month to month or year to year, and the terms of trade of a region which exports one primary product, or only a few, depend enormously not only on the general state of world demand, but on what its particular exports are.

This chapter has ranged superficially over an enormous territory in seeking to set out the main factors which govern prices, and which determine in the end the rates at which the specialized producer can exchange his output for other things. It is necessary to finish with a note of caution. The price-determining mechanisms which we have described as if they operated in the main independently for different kinds of good and service are, in fact, interconnected. A change in any price is likely to change, or at least to put pressure upon, hundreds of others, by three means—diverting demand, diverting productive resources, and altering the pattern of incomes. Behind the easy generalizations and descriptions of institutional arrangements to which this chapter has been limited stand the infinitely complex relationships which form the subject of the theory of value. These are complexities which we cannot pursue further here, but which anyone who tries seriously to understand the economic world must make it one of his main tasks to explore.

F

CHAPTER 6

Good and Poor Livings

Productivity, Prices, and Incomes

WE have seen that how good or how poor a living any group of people gets depends on how much it produces, and the terms of trade between what it has to sell and what it wants to buy. For self-sufficient groups, of course, the second factor does not exist; for large nations it has only a faction of the importance of the first factor. The United Kingdom normally exchanges about a quarter of its output of goods and services for other kinds of goods and services produced by residents in other countries; if therefore, its terms of trade deteriorated to the extent that twice as much of its exports as before had to be given for a unit of the things it imports, and if it still required the same amount of imports as before, its real income would fall by a quarter, because it would have to export half its output, instead of only a quarter, to buy its imports. In practice, its loss would be less than that, because the very reduction of its real income would reduce its import requirements somewhat, and, in addition, the worsened terms of trade would mean that it could now do better by using its efforts to satisfy directly some of the wants which it formerly paid it to satisfy by exporting and getting imports in exchange. Its real income would, therefore, fall by a good deal less than a quarter. If, however, its productivity in all lines of production were to fall by half, its real income would be nearly halved— even the improvement in its terms of trade which might accompany such a catastrophic event could do little to mitigate that consequence.

For a country which is still more nearly self-sufficient, like the United States, productivity counts for nearly everything and terms of trade for very little in determining the average standard of living. On the other hand, a family in an advanced economy exchanges a very high proportion of its output (which consists mostly of services) for things bought in the market. The rate of exchange between its services and the things it buys is therefore of nearly equal importance with its productivity in determining how good a living it gets.

We have looked in a general way at the main factors which influence productivity, and at the main factors which determine prices, and therefore terms of trade between one kind of goods or

services and others. It is time to apply what we have seen to the
further study of the reasons for the differences in levels of real
income which we find as we turn from a particular family, or an
occupational group in one country to its counterpart in another, or
from one occupational group to another in the same country.

If we had regard only to productivity, it might seem that the
average real income of workers in the radio industry in the United
States would be four times as great as the average income of
workers in the same industry in the United Kingdom, because
average physical productivities stand in that ratio. In the same way,
we might expect a baby-sitter in the United States to get the same
real income per hour as a baby-sitter in the United Kingdom,
because there is no presumption that productivities in that job are
at all different in the two countries. In practice, at any rate, things
certainly do not work out like that. American baby-sitters may not
be more efficient than British, but their pay per hour is about twice
the British in real purchasing-power, or three times as great if
converted into shillings at the current rate of exchange. The same
kind of relationship holds between American and British rates of
pay in many service industries, where there is not much evidence
of different real outputs per hour between the two countries. In
fact, this relationship is not very different from that which holds
between American and British pay rates in the manufacturing
industries, where, as we have seen, it is 'justified' by an American
rate of physical productivity per man-hour ranging from twice to
four times as great as the British. Generally speaking the ratio of
American to British rates of pay differs much less from one branch
of economic activity to another than does the ratio of American to
British physical outputs per person.

The Mutual Influence of Incomes
The reason for this is not hard to find. Within each of the two
countries concerned, there is a tendency for high incomes in any
important branch of activity which can be fairly easily entered to
pull up rates of pay in other branches of activity. Americans will
not consent to be domestic servants or clerks or garage hands at the
rates which are paid to people in those occupations in the United
Kingdom, because they (or, at any rate, many of them) have a
chance to go instead into manufacturing industry, where their high
productivity enables their employers to offer high wages or salaries,
and still to produce goods as cheaply as they can be produced in
other countries where both productivity and industrial rates of pay
are lower. In countries of lower industrial productivity such as the

United Kingdom, on the other hand, industrial workers could not be paid anything like as much as American industrial workers without making their products much dearer than competing American goods; the fact that industrial pay is lower in turn means that lower wages or salaries are paid to domestic servants or clerks or garage hands, even though they may be as efficient and productive as their American counterparts.

The general principles behind this can be stated perhaps more systematically in another way. Where the products of an industry are goods which do not cost very much (in relation to their value) to transport from one country to another, the existence of that industry in two or more countries implies that the money costs of production of a unit of the goods in question must be nearly the same in all of them—otherwise those where it was lower would drive those where it was higher out of this particular line of business. In such cases therefore, the average money income obtained by all the people directly and indirectly involved in making the product in question in a particular country as a reward for their part in making it must be proportional to their average efficiency. A particular kind of cotton cloth, say, is made both in the United Kingdom and the United States, which compete with one another in selling it either in each others' markets (though here, in practice, tariffs would complicate the issue) or in other countries. The costs of production of the British and American products, therefore (expressed either in pounds or dollars) must be more or less the same, or the industry could not survive in the dearer country, except for the aid of tariffs or other means of protection. If, then, the productivity of the American industry is twice as high as that of the British, in the sense that the output of these goods per person directly or indirectly involved is twice as great in the United States as in Britain, the average money receipts of these people from their contribution to the production of the cotton cloth must be twice as great in the United States as in Britain. Where, because they compete in the market, the money prices of the products of a number of countries are the same, the average money rewards of the people involved in making them must differ from country to country strictly in proportion to their average physical productivities.

This does, in fact, apply very largely to the industries which produce movable material goods (as opposed to services or fixed things like buildings). The prices of such goods differ from one country to another to extents which can be explained in terms of transport costs and the taxes or subsidies which governments may apply to them. Sometimes, of course, these natural and artificial costs of movement are large, in which case differences in cost of production may also be large—cameras, for instance, cost very much more in Britain than in Germany, and coal is much cheaper in most countries where it is mined than in others distant from any coalfield. Between countries which export a particular kind of commodity to others, however, there can be only small differences in the prices of the kinds of goods concerned; many kinds of manufactured goods cost about the same in all the great industrial countries, as (with some important exceptions due to government subsidies) do the principal agricultural products in the countries that export them. The relative levels of manufacturing wages (measured in some one currency) in the main industrial countries are thus quite a good guide to the relative physical productivities, on the average, of their respective manufacturing populations. American industrial wages (reckoned in shillings at the current rate of exchange) are $2\frac{1}{2}$ or 3 times as great as British, while the ratio of physical output per head in American industry to that in British industry, though it differs a good deal from one industry to another, probably averages between two and three, over manufacturing industry as a whole.

On the other hand, goods and services which cannot be at all easily transported over international frontiers may go on being produced in different countries at very different prices indefinitely; the forces of competition do relatively little to pull their prices into equality or to squeeze out production of them in countries where their costs are high. The cheapness of domestic service or house-building in Britain and India can do practically nothing to bring down the costs of these services in the United States. There is thus nothing to prevent their being made dear in America by the fact that the people engaged in supplying them have to be paid enough to keep them out of lucrative jobs in manufacturing industry, while they can be relatively cheap in the United Kingdom, and cheaper still in India, since these countries provide much less lucrative alternative occupations for domestic servants and builders.

One consequence of this is that, while the money wages of people engaged in producing goods which are transportable between countries tend to be proportional to their physical productivities, the same is not necessarily true of their real incomes. If American and British industrial workers spent their wages entirely upon manufactured products of the kinds that enter into international trade, the Americans would have real incomes nearly three times as great as the British. Large parts of wages, and of incomes generally, are, however, spent upon goods and services of kinds which are not traded internationally, and have therefore very little tendency to conform to the same money prices in different countries—house-room, entertainment, transport, and all kinds of services. Many of these are dearest in the countries which are most efficient at producing transportable goods, for the simple reason that this very efficiency makes labour dear, and that the scope for superior efficiency of labour in providing the services in question is generally less than in the production of transportable goods. It therefore very often happens that one country's superiority over another in the average level of real incomes—the average purchasing-power of wages, salaries, and other incomes in it—is a good deal less than its superiority in the average level of money incomes, reckoned at the current rate of exchange. American incomes, on the average, will buy not almost three times as much of the goods and services on which they are spent as would British incomes, but only about twice as much.[1]

This point has to be watched even more carefully when countries are compared in which the standards of living are still more widely different. Comparisons between India and the United States seem to indicate that the average real purchasing-power of Indian incomes is perhaps a tenth of a twelfth of that of American, whereas a comparison of the average rupee value of Indian incomes and the average dollar value of American, converted at the official rate of exchange, would make Indian incomes only a twentieth or a thirtieth as great as American. The difference arises mainly because such things as personal and domestic service are several times as dear in the United States as in India, reckoning at the official rate of exchange.

Inequality within the Economy

Broadly speaking, then, between countries which produce roughly similar things, average real income levels differ in proportion to the average physical productivities of labour in the countries concerned, in all the branches of production taken together. On the other hand, differences from one country to another in the relative productivities of labour in two occupations are not necessarily reflected as similar differences in the relative incomes earned in those occupations. High productivity in one occupation tends, as we have seen, to pull incomes in other occupations in the same country up. Nevertheless, it is one of the most obvious of all economic facts

---

[1] These comparisons relate to average income per occupied person. Since a rather higher proportion of the total population is occupied in the United Kingdom than in the United States, a comparison of incomes per head of the total population is somewhat less favourable to the United States.

that, within any country, incomes differ enormously from one occupation to another. It is true that some of the largest incomes in most countries—and hence some of the extremes of inequality—result from the ownership of property, but salaries and wages vary over a vast range—in the United Kingdom at present from well over £10,000 a year to under £200.

As Mrs Wootton points out in a recent book, these differences are so great that to talk about a tendency for incomes to be equalized between occupations may appear unrealistic. It is not so much that they tend to be equalized as that there is, in any country at any time, a set of barriers against equalization which tends to preserve a definite relation between the incomes of different groups of people. What is the nature of these barriers? To some extent, as Mrs Wootton maintains, they are purely traditional, and connected with the status which is accorded to the job in question. One is tempted to misquote Keats:

> 'Status is pay; pay, status; that is all
> We know on earth, and all we need to know.'

But to leave it at that is not very satisfactory. The degree of difference in pay which goes with a particular difference in status still requires to be explained, and so do differences in pay between occupations which are not recognized as corresponding to any difference of status—such as that between medical and non-medical members of the teaching staffs of British universities. What is paid for a particular man's services may seem to be determined immediately, at least, by nothing more definite than thinking what the dignity of his position demands (as with judges, ministers of the Crown, and chairmen of the boards of nationalized industries), but more usually—perhaps always, if one takes a long enough view—it must be related to what has to be paid to get that particular man's services (or the services of someone with similar qualifications) for that particular purpose. That this differs so much from one man (or a group of men with one kind of qualification) to another is a matter of the scarcity of that particular kind of qualification and the amount of competition for its services.

A very able administrator, of whom two or more firms believe that he is well worth a salary of £10,000 a year (in the sense that he could save them at least that much) is likely to get that salary, because one or more of the firms will be willing to offer it to him rather than lose him, providing that they see no hope of getting someone else as good for less money. But if there are plenty of men just as able, all of the posts where they could save, or make, £10,000 a year for their employers will be happily filled with them (or, less happily, with men who are thought as good and are not yet found out). Some of the men in question, therefore, will not be able to do better than occupy posts where they are thought to be worth much less—say £2,000 a year. And, since any of these would, presumably, go to a post where his services actually save the organization £10,000 a year or more if he were offered any substantial advance on £2,000, the latter sum, rather than £10,000 would in these circumstances tend to be the typical salary for men of this particular level of recognized (or assessed) ability. It is all a matter as economists are so fond of saying, of supply and demand—how many people manage to achieve qualifications which are recognized as being of this particular kind and quality, and how many jobs there are in which a man of this kind is thought to be worth *at least* some particular salary.

In the occupations where it is not customary, or easy, to assess what a particular man's services are worth in money (in the churches, and the universities, for instance), there is, nevertheless, generally a fairly clear idea of the qualities which are required for the post, and the salary offered will have to be at least sufficient to get men with the required qualities in competition with other employers, some of whom (such as commercial firms) will, probably, want them for purposes in which their worth can more easily be assessed in pounds, shillings and pence. In any kind of post, what a man is estimated to be worth—that is to say, what he is estimated to add to the product of the employing organization, or what he would be thus valued at by some other employer from whom it is deemed worth tempting him to stay away—is bound to set the upper limit to his wage or salary, and is likely to be quite closely related to it.

There is another objection which is often made to the statement that the incomes which people get in particular occupations, or particular kinds of post, are closely related to what they are estimated to be able to add to the product of the organization in which they are employed (or of some other organization from which they have to be diverted). This objection starts from the view that, if incomes were related as closely to ability as this would suggest, incomes in the community should share one characteristic with ability, as measured by examination marks, intelligence tests, and the like—namely, that the size of income most commonly met with —like the level of intelligence most commonly met with—should lie about midway between the highest and the lowest. Now, in fact, it is one of the most marked features of incomes, in every country for which we have any statistics, that the most usual income level is very much nearer the lower end of the range than the upper end. In the United Kingdom in 1956, for instance, there were some thousands over £10,000 a year (and even some over £20,000, though these probably came largely from property). There were, however, 10,400,000 incomes of between £250 and £600 a year, and 6,570,000 of less than £250, these two classes together containing about two-thirds of the total number of incomes in the country. The most commonly met income was thus one of a few hundred pounds a year—very much less than half-way between the smallest incomes (whatever they may have been) and the largest, which were well over £10,000. The distribution of income is clearly very different from the distribution of ability, as measured by any method so far used.

There are a number of possible explanations of this, at which it is possible only to hint here. It is possible that for any one occupation the productivity of different people in the population at large is distributed in much the same way as their intelligence—a relatively small number very good, a relatively small number very bad, and the greatest number about midway between the extremes. But if that is so, it does not in the least imply that incomes in that occupation are similarly distributed, even if income is closely connected with productivity, because the people who are worst at doing the particular thing—indeed perhaps all but the relatively few who are best—will not be in that occupation; they will probably be doing something else, at which they are better in relation to their fellows. Men who are tone-deaf are not to be found as piano-tuners. Even if there is a general tendency for the same people to be naturally good at everything or naturally bad at everything, the least able will tend to be in those occupations where the range of variation from the average is least (so that their natural disadvantage in comparison with others in the same occupation is least) and those who are best at everything will probably be in the lines where the range of variation is greatest and their superiority to their competitors therefore most marked. The mere fact that the natural range of abilities of people in general is widely different for different kinds of work—much wider for some than for others—thus tends to ensure that, so long as incomes have some connection with productivity, the upper incomes will be earned in occupations where abilities differ very much, and the lower incomes in those where they are much closer together. High incomes will thus themselves tend to be more 'spread out' than low incomes.

Another, and simpler, line of explanation is that in some occupations, notably in some which command high incomes, productivity of different people is not distributed in at all the same way as intelligence, or other measurable abilities. The 'productivity' of a barrister, for instance, consists of his ability to win cases—that is to say, to out-manoeuvre other barristers. The margin by which he does it does not matter very much; his clients will presumably be willing to pay a very large premium for mere superiority. In many of the positions in a competitive society, the winner 'takes all', which means that the man who is thought likely to 'win' commands an excess of salary over his rivals out of all proportion to his margin of superiority over them. People do not bet nine-tenths as much on a horse they expect to lose a race as they bet on the winner, on the ground they think it will lose only by one hundred yards in a race of 1,000.

These lines of explanation are not, of course, mutually exclusive, and there are doubtless others. The peculiar, lop-sided distribution of incomes which appears in all the economies about which we know anything is not really hard to explain in a way consistent with a close connection between income and productivity. The trouble is, rather, that we do not know enough to enable us to choose between different kinds of explanation, or to assign degrees of relative importance to them. The distribution of income between individuals and occupations, which is clearly one of the most important features of any economy, is one with which the economists have not really done very well so far.

CHAPTER 7

How Economies Grow

so far, we have been looking at the essential processes and mechanisms by which economies live, and trying to account for the widely varying livings they provide, both on the average and for different families within a given economy. At this point it may be useful to recall that, as was mentioned in Chapter 1, economies, like living things, grow, and to look at the processes by which they do it.

Economic growth is a subject which, after a long period of neglect, has in this generation attracted a vast amount of attention, and about which a large literature has grown up. In this chapter (as, indeed, in others in this book) we can give no more than a sketch of the main processes and issues concerned. For a more fundamental discussion of the factors which determine growth the reader is referred to Professor Lewis's great book *The Theory of Economic Growth,* and for a survey of nearly everything which can be said in quantitative terms about it to Mr Colin Clark's no less great work *The Conditions of Economic Progress.* Here we shall draw heavily upon these two sources.

First, what do we mean by the growth of an economy? What, in other words, is the dimension of it upon which we fix our attention in discussing its growth? Some writers (including Professor Lewis) have chosen to concentrate upon the real income which the economy provides, on the average, for its people. While this is of the first importance, however, in relation to the material well-being and the whole way of life of the people in question (and we shall return to it shortly), it is perhaps more natural to judge growth by reference to something which measures the total size of the economy—and for this purpose the most obvious criterion is its total real product or income.

The Products of the Great Powers

Just as the development of average real income per head in an economy is of key importance in any discussion of its social life, so the development of its total product, considered in relation to the corresponding development in other economies, is of key importance for understanding one important aspect of political history, namely

91

the history of changes in national power. Unfortunately, data for estimating real national products do not extend far back into the past for most countries. It can be roughly estimated that, about the end of the Napoleonic Wars, the United Kingdom, France, the United States, and perhaps Russia had national products of not dissimilar size, small of course by modern standards, and small also, it would seem, by comparison with such populous countries as India or China, or (to look further back) with what the product of the Roman Empire had been at its height. By 1850, the British product had doubled, the French nearly doubled, the American nearly quadrupled. By 1870, the British national product was not very far from having doubled again, and was perhaps 70 per cent. greater than the French. The United States, after the setback of the Civil War, was probably not much ahead of the United Kingdom in output. Russia, which, like the United States had grown territorially as well as in other ways, had a product as great as or greater than the American. Meanwhile the new Germany had arisen with a product intermediate in size between the French and the British. The leading great powers of the later nineteenth century were for the first time comparable in their total products with what the Roman Empire may have produced, with a population perhaps as large as the Russian population of 1870; they were also approaching the magnitudes of output realized (with much bigger populations) by India and China in their own time.

After 1870, the United States began to show a commanding lead in this race. Whereas by 1900 the British and German products were more than doubled, the French nearly doubled, and the Russian raised by perhaps 60 or 70 per cent., the American had more than trebled—it by then stood at something like double the German. These trends continued (though with some fall in the British growth rate) until 1914, when the American real product was, apparently, more than twice the British, the German, or the Russian, or more than four times the French. The war of 1914-18 accelerated this relative advance of the United States; by 1929 her product was some 80 per cent. higher than in 1914; it was over four times as great as the German national product and nearly four times the British, the increases in both of these since before the war having been modest. The French product, though it had risen by some 50 per cent., had fallen in relation to the American. On the other hand, Japan had become one of the major economic powers of the world, with a product which had, at least since 1900, increased even faster than the American—in those twenty-nine years it had risen three-and-a-third-fold (against an American increase of just under threefold), and by the nineteen-thirties was about as big as the national product of France. Of the countries for which there are adequate estimates, only Norway, New Zealand and Canada seem to have shown rates of growth about as great as the Japanese or the American in this period.

The 'thirties were a period of stagnation in the United States, France, and a number of other countries, while the economies of the United Kingdom, Germany, and the Soviet Union were growing rapidly after the early part of the decade. American predominance over the economic scene was therefore less marked on the eve of the second world war than it had been ten years before, but this was largely a matter of depression—under-use of available resources rather than lack of productive capacity—and the demands of war brought output up to the limits of capacity in all economies which were not too dislocated by enemy attack or occupation. The American product at the peak of the war effort was probably over three times as great as that of Greater Germany (including Austria and the Sudetenland)—a product which was probably appreciably greater than that of Russia and perhaps 50 per cent. greater than that of the United Kingdom at the time.

We come, finally, to the nineteen-fifties, in which up to the time of writing economic growth has been more widespread and, for the world as a whole, certainly more rapid than ever before. The two outstanding features of the time are the continued predominance of the United States economy and the rapid recent growth (to a size already beyond that of any national economy except the American) of the Soviet Union. American predominance needs little emphasis; the output of goods and services in the United States is on some reckonings nearly a third of the world total, and on some a good deal more. Moreover, the American rate of growth is still impressive. Over the years since something approaching full employment was attained in 1941, it has averaged about the same as in the great period from 1870 to 1929, when the real national product was roughly trebling each thirty years. In spite of the great depression and the stagnation of the 'thirties, output had doubled in twenty-three years from 1929.

Taken over long periods, the growth of Russian economy has been less impressive than that of the American. Its product did not reach treble the 1913 level until about forty years later—in the early 'fifties. This period, however, contains two disastrous wars and (at the beginning of the 'thirties) a great crisis in agricultural production occasioned by the incorporation of the peasants in collective farms. If we take the shorter periods in which production was neither being reduced by these events nor simply making a recovery back to the old level from them, we see some very remarkable growth-rates. Between 1934 and 1940, there was an increase of about 50 per cent. in output, which amounts to 7 per cent. a year. Between 1949 and 1955, the average rate of increase seems to have been much the same as this, though there is some evidence that it fell in the later years of the period. It is impossible to say whether such rates of growth can be kept up over long periods, or whether there is in them an element of recovery to efficient and smooth working after a period of great upheaval. All that can be said is that, over two short periods the Soviet economy has grown at something approaching twice the annual rate which the American economy has maintained (apart from the depressed nineteen-thirties) ever since 1870. By 1955, the Russian output was probably in the region of twice the British, which was the next national product in order of size. But the American product was probably still between two-and-a-half and three times as great as the Russian, which had been about equal to it—and bigger than that of any other great power—in 1870.

The Growth of Population

This sketch may serve to illustrate the wide variety, and in some cases the astonishing rapidity, of economic growth rates in the modern world. We must look for causes. One cause of growth in the output of an economy which comes at once to mind is increase in its population, particularly its working population, which has been a feature of most of the national economies of the world in the last hundred years or more.

Sometimes growth of population has accounted for the whole of the growth of an economy's product in, at any rate, the simple, arithmetical sense that population has increased while average output per head has stayed constant. This may well have been substantially true of India in much of the nineteenth century, for instance. In other cases population growth has accounted, in this simple sense, for the greater part of the growth of the product. This was probably true of the United States from the beginning of the nineteenth century (or earlier) until the first world war. In the first half of the nineteenth century, indeed, the rate of growth of population (at something over $2\frac{1}{2}$ per cent. a year) was probably more than twice as great as the rate of growth of output per head. Later in the century output per head grew faster and the percentage (though not the absolute) rate of growth of population declined, but population increase still remained the larger source of expansion

in the real national product until the nineteen-twenties. The United
Kingdom has never experienced such a rapid population growth as
the United States—in the last third of the nineteenth century
working population in Great Britain grew at about 1½ per cent. a
year, which was about half the rate of growth of total output. Here,
it was output per head which fell first; from 1899 to 1913 what
increases there were in the real product were almost entirely due to
population growth. When output per head grew again after the first
world war, however, it in turn became responsible for most of the
growth in the national product; the working population has, since
then, been increasing only very slowly. In general, it can be said that
the rates of increase of product per head which have been shown to
be possible in the most rapidly-developing countries in the twentieth
century, like Russia in its two great spurts, or Japan between 1914
and 1929, are considerably greater than the rate at which any large
country's population can be expected to grow.

Before we leave population growth as a contributor to the
expansion of an economy, however, there are two questions at
which we should glance. What have been the causes of the rapid
population growths—so very rapid compared with those of most
earlier times—which have made large contributions to the story?
And how have these rapid growths of population taken place
without actually reducing output per head—generally, indeed, to the
accompaniment of increases in it?

These questions seem easiest to answer for the new countries—
North America, Australia, or New Zealand. The population of these
countries have grown partly by immigration. The contribution which
this has made is not, however, usually the major one. In the early
nineteenth century, when the United States population was increasing at over 2½ per cent. a year, the excess of births over deaths was
more than twenty times as great as the net gain by immigration. In
the decades just before the first world war, immigration was
responsible for nearly half the American population growth—for
about 1 per cent. increase in the population each year, that is to
say—but it never became the major partner. Perhaps it is only in
Canada in the early nineteen-hundreds, and New Zealand in the
eighteen-seventies that it has predominated over natural increase in
a rapidly-growing country. All the same, immigration of people with
high natural rates of increase is clearly the reason for the rapid
expansion of the population in the countries in question, and there
is not much mystery about the reason for the immigration—people
went to the new lands because they thought they would be more
free there in matters of politics or religion than in the Old

World; but most of all because they thought they would get better livings.

Why the immigrants into the new countries increased rapidly by the excess of births over deaths among them is essentially the same question as why high rates of natural increase are found in any communities—as they are found in very large parts of the modern world. Lest we should take this for granted as a permanent state of affairs, it is worth remembering that for most of recorded time the growth of populations has been slow. For the first sixteen centuries of the Christian era it is believed to have been not substantially more, and possibly very much less, than one per *thousand* of the population of the world as a whole each year. Latterly it has been one per *cent.*—at least ten times as great. It is plain from a very simple calculation that a growth-rate as fast as this is bound to be temporary, if one takes the long view of human prospects. A one per cent. a year rate of growth would cover the whole land surface of the globe with inhabitants as thickly as the County of London is covered now in less than a thousand years.

The causes of rapid population growth are various, complex, and frequently little understood. The great accelerations of the last century or two, however, have mainly been traceable to fairly rapid falls in death rates, associated sometimes with greater cleanliness, sometimes with better food, sometimes with the retreat of important diseases, like the bubonic plague, for reasons which are often obscure. In the last generation or two falls in death rate have been increasingly due to public health measures, like the eradication of malaria by the use of D.D.T., or to improved medical practice and the use of the new specific drugs and antibiotics. To some extent the factors which reduce death rate are likely to go with, or are part of, improvements in the average real income per head. Better feeding, clothing, and housing are almost sure to lower mortality, other things being equal. In any particular increase of real income it may be that one of these three factors deteriorates; a shift of the population into towns, for instance, generally goes with increasing income, and in some periods towns have been so much more insanitary than the country that a rise in death rates has resulted. In general, however, rising income per head is likely to promote lower death rates.

It is true that higher average income promotes lower birth rates as well. The causes of reduction in birth rates are more complex, and certainly more obscure, than those of reduction in death rates, but in general they are bound up with improvements in the standard of living, or with urbanization which usually goes with it. Since, however, rising income seems to take longer to lower birth rates than to lower death rates, rapid economic development tends to produce a large gap between the two—that is to say, a high rate of natural increase, for two, three or four generations. Thereafter, the fact that it becomes much harder to reduce death rates when nearly everybody lives to a ripe age tends to let reduction in birth rate catch up, and the rate of natural increase falls again. It is no accident, however, that the early stages of rapid development, carrying with them substantial improvements in the standard of living, also tend to be times of rapid population-growth.

But this raises the second question which we have mentioned: how is it that a rapid population-growth does not itself extinguish improvement in the standard of living, and, indeed, lead to a fall? If the non-human resources and the technical knowledge of the economy in question did not increase, we should certainly expect some such unhappy outcome: smaller supplies of the other factors of production in relation to labour would lower the average product per head. Indeed, this would act as a controlling mechanism, keeping the standard of living from rising permanently; every time it rose at all, population would presently increase to wipe out the improvement. For this reason many of the economists of the early nineteenth century believed that average income could never rise above a level which, for the wage-earner, meant bare subsistence.

It is probable that this unhappy state of affairs has existed in, for instance, India and China over considerable periods (perhaps most of the eighteenth and nineteenth centuries in India). But it is clear why it did not exist in, say, the United States or Australia. Resources were not effectively limited. Land in use was increased at least as fast as the agricultural population; mineral deposits were opened up as demand for them grew without recourse having to be had to new sources which were much poorer or harder to work than the old ones. Moreover, capital and knowledge also increased, but the effects of this can perhaps be better seen in the older countries, where the supply of natural resources were less extensible.

Why, then, did population increase not lower income per head in these older countries, like Great Britain where it was less rapid than in the new countries, but still spectacular? It is true that some agricultural resources and great resources of coal and iron ore were opened up in the course of the nineteenth century, but the extent to which this meant using poorer land, deeper-lying (and sometimes thinner) seams, and less rich ores, was considerable. The greater part, by far, of the reason why production was able to increase faster than population in Great Britain and similar countries (like

Germany, the Low Countries, and Switzerland) is to be found in the growth of technical knowledge, and the growth of capital at a faster rate than population.

The development of such countries, where resources of certain kinds were very strictly limited, has depended also upon the possibility of international trade which we shall discuss in Chapters 9 and 10. This possibility means that either production can be concentrated on the things which require little of the scarcest factors (manufactured goods, for instance, if land is scarce), while other kinds of finished goods are imported, or some of the product can be used to buy imports of the scarcest factors, if these are mobile, as raw materials and capital are. On a smaller scale, but even more strikingly, local specialization makes possible enormously high rates of population growth in towns, which may produce nothing requiring much land, and may also import virtually all the power and new materials and even much of the capital required for their manufacturing and service industries.

Technical Progress and Knowledge

Whether population is increasing or not, technical knowledge and capital are the great twin agents of improvement in average production per head. The relations between them are close, and often hard to disentangle. Every net addition to capital equipment requires more knowledge, in the sense of additional people knowing how to work with and look after the additional 'produced means of production', whether these are factories, railways, or livestock. Similarly, changes in the physical form or design of capital goods, brought about by replacing old ones with new, require new technical knowledge to be imparted to those who will work with them, besides needing, of course, the new technical knowledge for producing them. It is equally true that new knowledge of how to satisfy wants nearly always requires new equipment to make it effective—sometimes new kinds of equipment in addition to those which already exist, but usually new equipment which can take the place of some which already exists. Normally the increase of technical knowledge makes each 'generation' of new equipment for an industry more efficient than its predecessor in the sense that it makes possible a lower cost of production of the product, if we measure these costs for each generation in money units equal to (say) an hour's wages at the time.

Perhaps we should look at this point rather more closely. Progress of this kind in relation to, for instance, motor cars may mean any of a number of things. It may mean that, to get a thousand motor cars produced each year, we require fewer men at work in all the industries concerned (not only the motor industry, but all the industries which supply it and maintain its equipment, and all the industries which serve *them*, and so on). Or it may mean that, while we do not require appreciably fewer men, we require an outfit of capital goods of all kinds which is smaller in cost than before. Or it may mean that the requirement of both men and capital is reduced —this seems to be the case in some instances where automatic machine tools linked by 'transfer machines' are installed in the place of sets of separate machine tools. Economists are accustomed to thinking to more advanced methods of production as requiring fewer men but a bigger outfit of capital—the extra interest charge on the capital being less than the saving in direct and indirect labour costs. This replacement of man-power by plant and machinery is, indeed, one of the common modes of development, and successive 'generations' of capital goods are better and better at it. But it is also quite common for an invention or a development in the design of equipment to save both man-power and capital. Finally, in thinking about the ways in which greater knowledge promotes progress in the production of motor cars, we must not forget improvements in the design and performance of the motor cars themselves, as distinct from improvements in the methods of executing the design. Technical progress is far from simple.

There is, however, a fairly clear distinction to be made between two kinds of task which face economies in improving their production per head by means of knowledge and capital. One is the task of the economy which is already in the forefront of technical progress, the other that of the truly 'underdeveloped' economy; the one which is technically far behind. The latter can, *in favourable circumstances*, raise its output per head faster than the former, simply because of the increasing efficiency of capital goods, and the improving design of products, to which we have just referred. There is a greater improvement when one puts in modern machinery in place of machinery designed in 1900 than when one puts it in place of machinery designed in 1935; more advantage in replacing gas-lamps by sodium vapour lamps than in replacing electric filament lamps by them.

In principle, a very advanced economy might find itself able to improve its standard of living only as fast as it could advance the frontiers of technical knowledge, its supply of capital and its ability to train its people being, let us suppose, sufficient to enable it to keep up with the best known methods in every branch of production. This is in some degree a question-begging a statement; which of the known methods was, in fact 'the best' would depend upon the rate of interest, and so upon what the supply of capital actually was—but we can perhaps ignore this complication for the present purpose.

It is clear that the more backward economy is not limited in its rate of progress by having to wait for research and development; plenty of technical information on how it can improve its productive methods—and improve them drastically—exists ready-made. Other factors, of course, limit the rate at which it can apply this knowledge, and they may be such as either to permit it to progress faster than an advanced economy, moving with the technological frontier, or to limit it to a very much slower rate of advance. Japan and the Soviet Union have achieved their rapid rates of progress largely by moving up from far behind to technological frontiers which had been advanced mainly by other pioneers. India and China have been prevented by other factors from making much progress (until very recently) towards technical frontiers far beyond their existing practice. No economy can claim to have been wholly up to the frontiers of technological progress, but the United States has been near enough to them during most of the last two generations for the rate of advance of knowledge through research (American and other) to have played a very important—perhaps the predominant—part in setting the rate of increase in its productivity.

What, then, determines the rate of growth of technological knowledge? Clearly, it is the extent (and success) of a whole complex of research activity, beginning with pure science and ending often with development of commercial processes on quite a large scale in pilot plants. The scale on which this work goes on in an advanced economy nowadays is considerable; on the other hand it is still not very big in relation to the total product of the economy—less than 1 per cent. of it in both the United Kingdom and the United States, if we exclude defence research—and it was, until very recently, much smaller; it has probably quadrupled in the United Kingdom in the last generation. How much research is done depends on a large number of factors, of which the most important is probably the realization in governmental quarters, among the directors of industry, and in the quarters which control education, that this is a matter of great moment for the community as a whole. The spectacular successes of science and technology, and the mounting evidence of their contribution to welfare in peace and survival in war have gradually fostered this realization in most countries; hence a good deal of the cumulative or 'snowball' character which technical and economic progress has shown.

We come now to the conditions which enable the existing technological knowledge to be applied in an economy. The first of these is that it should be available, in the sense that it is not kept secret from the people who might use it in the economy concerned. A great deal—it is impossible to say how much—is, in principle available to anyone in the form of published literature, though some discoveries are retained by the firms which make them as 'trade secrets', and especially in the field of atomic energy this has recently happened to some of the output of government research as well.

But for discoveries to be available in a fuller sense, there must be people who have not only the will to know about them, but the scientific training to understand them also, and shortage of such people has certainly been a factor limiting the application of new techniques in the United Kingdom; far more so in the underdeveloped countries. Moreover, acquaintance with the right technical literature is not enough; it is generally necessary, before a new process can be transferred to a country, for people from that country to have extensive practical experience of the process, or else for foreigners who have such experience to be brought in.

To this need for technologists with the essential 'know-how' we must add a need for training much of the supervisory and the skilled or semi-skilled parts of the labour force which is involved—how much training is necessary, and how difficult it is depending very much upon the extent to which there are people with experience of roughly similar kinds of work, and on the standard of general education. It is difficult to introduce factory industry of any kind, for instance, if very few of the potential workpeople have any previous experience of it, or if there are not enough qualified candidates for the jobs which demand literacy. And productivity is generally for quite a long time much lower where the labour-force is newly recruited to a factory industry than where it can be recruited from similar, or even not so similar factory trades—the rate of labour turnover in a newly-recruited factory labour force is, for one thing, usually very high.

All these difficulties can, of course, be overcome, but to overcome them in a newly developing country demands both time and a large expenditure on general and technical education. Not only does an advanced economy devote 3 per cent. or more of its resources to providing and staffing schools and universities; it keeps in them a number of pupils equal to a third or a quarter of its gainfully occupied population, who by the standards of former times are old enough to be gainfully occupied themselves.

Capital and Income

So much for the diffusion of knowledge and skills which is essential in applying technical progress. Another essential, as we have seen, is capital. It follows from what has been said about the increasing efficiency of capital equipment that a country with a stationary population, or even a slowly increasing one, can increase its output per head without increasing its capital, the latter being measured by its cost of production at constant factor-prices. So long as each generation of equipment is replaced by something better designed and more effective in relation to its real cost, the total productive power of the capital stock will go on increasing. Indeed, the United Kingdom seems to have managed to raise output per head since the nineteen-twenties with very little net increase in its real capital stock within the country until the nineteen-fifties.

Needless to say, this improvement depends upon the replacement of old capital goods with new ones. The frequency with which this is done varies a good deal from one economy to another, even as between broadly similar industries; American industry is said to replace its plant and machinery more frequently than British industry does. This frequency of replacement (provided that the new equipment put in is always of the latest design) naturally affects the average age and thus the average efficiency of the capital goods which are to be found in the economy at any given time. If the average frequency of replacement of machines of a certain kind is once in ten years, and about the same number are replaced each year, then the average age of the machines in operation will always be about five years, or, more generally, half the average time for which a machine is kept. But it is worth noting that, unless the rate of improvement in the design of capital equipment is changing, the frequency of replacement does not directly affect the rate of progress; the economy which replaces its equipment infrequently will appear old-fashioned, but its productivity will not on that account necessarily be growing more slowly than that of an economy which replaces more frequently.

It seems from the combined experience of a number of countries that, for any given quantity of capital per head, income per head was about 60 per cent. higher in 1938 than in 1913—a growth in the 'effectiveness' of capital by about $1\frac{1}{2}$ per cent. a year. Nevertheless, growth in the quantity of capital per head, as distinct from improvements in its quality through periodic replacement, is a further important factor in the raising of average incomes. And, more obviously, expansion of capital to keep up with increases in the population is necessary if there is to be any substantial improvement in average productivity (or even to prevent a fall in average productivity), especially, as we have noted, if the supply of other resources is not matching that of labour.

How much capital is required to produce an extra unit of income—the 'capital-output ratio'—is a magnitude which has occupied a very prominent place in discussion in recent years because of the great and widespread concern with the planning of economic development, to which it has an obvious relevance. It is however, one about which it is exceedingly hard to generalize fruitfully, partly because statistics of capital and its accumulation are often hopelessly inadequate, partly because here, even more than in most fields, circumstances alter cases. What a given increment of capital will add to income depends on the industry in which it is invested, the technique which that industry uses (there often being a range of possible techniques suited to different economic circumstances), and how far labour to work with the new capital is newly drawn into production, how far diverted from activities in which it was already making some contribution, large or small, to the economy's total output.

In the United Kingdom in 1954, the ratio of capital used by various industries to value of the work they contributed to the national product (or, more precisely, the value they added by their work to their materials and power) ranged from over 9 in oil refining to about 1½ in shipbuilding and pottery. For British manufacturing industry as a whole it is about 2·8. For railways (including their workshops) the ratio is probably about 12; for houses and roads it is higher still, and for the service trades which contribute such large parts of the national output it is no doubt much lower than for any manufacturing industry.

To ascertain the amount of capital required altogether (not just in one industry) for producing given increments in various kinds of output is much harder, because to increase output of any kind of good, provided that all the economy's capital is already occupied, and remains occupied, will call for an extension of capacity in practically every branch of activity in the economy. An increase in, say, clothing production demands not only more capacity in outfitters' shops, clothing factories, textile mills, and dyeworks, and also more growing of wool and cotton (or more manufacture of things to export in exchange for them); it demands in addition more output of textile and other machinery, of iron and steel, bricks and cement, machinery for making textile and cement-making equipment, and so on indefinitely. Calculations to determine the total ultimate capital and labour requirements for different products in the United States have been made by Professor Leontief; they show ratios of capital equipment and stocks needed (throughout the economy) to value of product emerging per year which vary from less than one for banking services or radio broadcasts, through values of between $1\frac{1}{2}$ and $2\frac{1}{2}$ for a great many manufactured goods (clothes, radio sets, motor cars, and most kinds of machinery), to three or more for most food and tobacco products, about four for electric power, and over five for telephone calls. Although this range is smaller than that over which the capital-output ratios of *industries* (as distinct from kinds of final product) are scattered, it is quite big enough to show that the capital-output ratio for a whole economy must depend a good deal upon what it chooses to produce.

As for the range of possible methods of producing any given kind of goods, it is sometimes immense. Indian data suggest that handloom weavers use capital which is worth only a small fraction of the value of their annual output, whereas weaving as a factory industry requires capital equal to about two years' output. The range of methods which would be regarded as practicable in a developing country is, in most manufacturing industries, very much narrower than this, but in agriculture, at least, it is often very wide (depending on the degree in which the land is improved or irrigated and the extent of mechanization), and the same is true of civil engineering and public works, with the choice they present between shovels and bulldozers.

The last of the reasons mentioned above for differences in the capital-output ratio between one case of economic development and another was that the extra capital is sometimes used with labour which is available without reducing the man-power which works with existing capital, whereas in other cases this is not so. Capital is only one of the factors of production, and how much extra product flows from an increase in it must depend greatly on the extra supplies of the other factors which are available. A country with a rapidly increasing working population and with abundant untapped natural resources would be expected to show a lower ratio of extra capital to extra output than one with a stationary working population and with all its natural resources rather fully used.

There does, indeed, seem to be some evidence that the ratio has been consistently lower in the United States (with plenty of natural resources) than in Japan; very often, however, the differences one would expect to see on these grounds are masked by bigger differences due to other causes; especially to the fact that economies at different stages of development naturally invest in different kinds of production, which may show such immensely different capital-output ratios. Thus, for instance, the great periods of population increase and of opening-up of natural resources have sometimes coincided with (indeed, have demanded) a heavy concentration of investment in railways, roads, and houses, for which, as we have seen, the ratio is very high. This was certainly true of the United Kingdom in the middle, and the United States in the last quarter of the nineteenth century. On the other hand, the United Kingdom since the second world war has been able to fall back upon increasingly intensive use of its transport facilities without adding much to them, and to put a high proportion of its investment into industrial equipment for which the capital-output ratio is low. But, against this, a high proportion of the new British equipment in recent years has necessarily gone to equip men who were already producing something before they got it, as opposed to equipping a net addition to the labour force, and to that extent the increment in total production for which it has been responsible is less than it would have been in an economy with a more rapidly increasing labour force.

All things considered, it is perhaps surprising that the capital-output ratio for a whole economy, especially the marginal ratio (the ratio of *extra* capital to *extra* output), should be sufficiently stable to be interesting. Nevertheless, for some economies which have been expanding either over long periods, or at full stretch over short periods, it appears to be so. The best way of calculating it is to divide the average proportion of income which is added to capital each year over the period in question (i.e. average net investment in the country as a proportion of national income) by the average annual rate of increase of real income. A calculation of this kind gives values of about three for the United States in the last quarter of the nineteenth century; for the United Kingdom in the same period the data are very sparse, but the indication is that the capital-output ratio lay, on the average, between three and four. For the United Kingdom in the first half of the nineteen-fifties it seems to have had the low value of two (perhaps because of the concentration on industrial equipment referred to above), while for most west European economies it was apparently nearer to three (or four in the Netherlands and Finland). In India under the first Five-Year Plan it proved to be less than two. In the Soviet Union it seems to be about three. Considering the vast differences of circumstances between these economies, the similarities between their marginal capital-output ratios are perhaps more impressive than the difference.

The Supply of Savings

The next question about the factors which govern the rate of growth is what determines the supply of capital in an economy. The short answer is that this depends on the rate at which the economy can either save from its own income or borrow from abroad, and we must look quickly at each of these possibilities.

Saving, as we have seen in Chapter 3 may be done either by private households, enterprises, or governments. In the most backward economies, enterprises which are really distinct from households are few, governments are weak or economically unenterprising, and households are generally either too poor to save more than a very little or, where they are better off, accustomed to spending on services and conventional luxuries what they might in principle save. Generally, therefore, the poorest economies save little; not more than 5 per cent. of their income, and sometimes much less. Five per cent. is, for instance, about the proportion of Indian income which was saved until the first Five-Year Plan.

At the other end of the scale, the richest countries save (in addition to providing for the maintenance of their existing capital goods) anything from about 7 to 19 per cent. of their income—the United Kingdom has recently been near to the bottom of this range, Western Germany and Canada near the top, and the United States in the middle. In the last quarter of the nineteenth century the United Kingdom was probably saving about the same proportion of its income as the United States saves now.

In most communities it seems that, at any time, well-to-do families save a higher proportion of their incomes than poorer families—the rise in proportion of income saved with increase in income is quite steep. This might lead one to expect that, as any community manages to increase the average real incomes of its members, the proportion of total income which is saved will increase. As we have mentioned, however, this has not proved to be true of the United States or the United Kingdom (or, apparently, of most other advanced countries) over the last two or three generations, and the increase in armament (and other government) expenditure cannot be a full explanation— the average real incomes left to families even after they have paid their taxes to the government have risen immensely. There is, indeed, not yet agreement on the full explanation of the non-increase of the proportion of income saved in such countries. Probably the explanation is complex; for the present purpose, however, it is enough to note that there has been, over a long period, a fairly steady fall in the proportion which families have saved (i.e. a rise in the proportion which they have spent on consumption) out of any

given real income. It would be surprising if the introduction of new
and more attractive outlets for expenditure—safe and easy means of
public transport, private motor cars, television receivers, vacuum
cleaners, holiday camps—had not something to do with this; but so,
no doubt, have many other factors.

The richest countries are not the only ones which save high proportions of their incomes. Just as they, as we have seen, already had
high propensities to save (in some cases even higher than they have
now) when their average incomes per head were only half or a
quarter of what they are today, so there are still relatively poor but
progressive countries which save proportions of their incomes as
high as are to be found in any of the richest. Indeed, the Soviet
Union and most other European Communist countries seem in
recent years to have saved nearly twice as high a proportion of their
income as has the United States—probably something like 20 per
cent. of it if the reckoning is done by the methods usual in the West.
Moreover, Japanese saving reached about 13 per cent. of income in
the nineteen-thirties and again recently, and the Federation of
Rhodesia and Nyasaland has in the last few years probably achieved
the highest rate of any country in the world.

Professor Lewis points out that the transition of an initially poor
country from a low rate of saving to a high one is the central factor
in economic development, the heart of an industrial revolution. How
does it come about? There seem to be two main ways, which are,
however, not mutually exclusive. One is for enterprises to begin to
make profits, out of which they save a large part; the other is for
the public authorities to collect by taxation (or sometimes to get by
creating new money) more than they spend on current purposes.
This surplus they can either use themselves to pay for new capital
goods or make available (by repaying debt, for instance) to private
enterprises who want it for capital purposes.

The first of these ways—profit-making and saving by enterprise—
is the 'classical' method which featured in the United Kingdom, the
United States, and other countries where governments did not play
very active parts in the early stages of modern economic development—though in most countries other than the United Kingdom
they helped to increase profits by protecting enterprises of some
kinds against foreign competition. The essential point about this
growth under private enterprise is that a considerable part of income
should be concentrated in the hands of people who want, and know
how, to use it for productive investment. Landowners, who claim
the largest incomes in many undeveloped countries, often do not
satisfy this condition, though at certain times, as in England in the

eighteenth century, they have played an important part by saving a portion of their income to invest in agricultural improvements. But people who have made their incomes from enterprises of their own in trade or industry, know (or think they know) very well how to make more by investing more, especially in their existing businesses. They have therefore strong incentives to save for productive investment. Thus, once they begin to be generally successful, their incomes tend to grow faster than those of other well-to-do people whose propensity to save is lower, and the proportion of the whole economy's income which is saved rises. Some 40 or 50 per cent. of British savings has consisted in recent years of the undistributed profits of companies, and a large part of personal savings (which have been 30 or 40 per cent. of the total) must also have been made by people whose incomes came to a substantial extent from profits and dividends. Profits are still the source of most savings, though thrift is more widespread in developed economies like that of the United Kingdom today than in those which are at an earlier stage of development.

The outstanding example of saving by the government out of the proceeds of taxation is provided by the Soviet Union. Until the last few years, indeed, nearly all the saving there took the form of revenue—mainly from the turnover tax on consumers' goods—which the state allocated to investment purposes, as distinct from administration or armaments. In recent years, however, there has been a considerable change, at least in the nominal sources of saving. The prices of goods (before turnover tax), which were formerly fixed so as to correspond fairly closely in aggregate to the costs of production paid out by enterprises, have now come to allow a considerable margin of profit, most of which is, in effect, taken in taxation, but some part of which (amounting in 1955 to about 30 per cent. of all savings) the enterprises are allowed to keep for approved capital purposes. Personal savings, mostly placed in savings banks or subscribed to state loans, have also become quite important, accounting for a further 18 per cent. of total savings. The remaining 52 per cent. is still allocated by the government out of its revenue, but that revenue itself now consists, as to nearly a third, of sums taken from enterprises' profits, the rest coming mainly from the turnover tax. The change is not really a very profound one, since the profits in question are not in principle available (as are those of privately-owned enterprises in other countries) for distribution to households, and it does not matter much in that case whether the excess of the prices of consumers' goods over their cost of production is described as turnover tax or as profits. It is out of that excess, apart from the contribution of private savings, that the great expansion of the Russian economy is essentially financed.

Capital from Abroad

We must now turn to borrowing from abroad as a source of capital for economies. In the whole course of their development, it has generally been a much smaller source than internal saving, but there have been cases in which it has been very important even by the roughest quantitative test, and there are few if any in which it has had no importance at all. There are two immediate reasons for external borrowing; one is that it may be the easiest way of getting hold of capital funds at all, and the other that it may be the easiest way of getting foreign currency with which to buy imports which are needed for development. These may be looked at in turn.

Poor and undeveloped economies, as we have seen, save very little, and that little, moreover, is not necessarily easily available to the people, or the authorities, who may want capital for productive investment. There is often no capital market in such countries where a loan can be floated, and sometimes no system of savings banks through which savings are collected up. Where (at a rather more advanced stage of development) such facilities exist, it is usually dear to borrow through them, because the rates of interest are high as a result of the scarcity of savings and the eagerness of many people (especially peasants) to borrow when they fall on hard times —when crops fail, for instance. It is therefore often much cheaper and easier to borrow in the great capital markets of the highly developed countries than to raise capital locally in less developed parts of the world—provided (and it is a crucial proviso) that the borrower is in a position to command confidence.

Where he has done so, it has usually been for one of two main reasons—because he is a government which appears sufficiently stable and efficient to be able to raise the necessary interest and instalments of repayment on the loan through taxation (this is a great deal easier, for a long time, at any rate, than raising the necessary capital itself out of taxation), or because he already has connections in the great capital markets and, perhaps, investments which have already proved sound over a considerable period. Colonial regimes, though they have not always been economically enterprising, have usually provided readier access to capital than the countries in question would have enjoyed, in their early days of development, if they had been independent. Lenders in the mother country generally have confidence in the solvency of colonial governments, and people or organizations from the mother country who start enterprises in colonial territories often have a toe in the door of the capital market back at home. Apart from colonial and similar political connections, purely commercial connections have also promoted easy international borrowing; it is no accident that the British merchant bankers, whose business was partly to know the credit-worthiness of traders in particular overseas countries, came to be the main agents of the enormous British long-term lending to those countries in the later part of the last century and the first generation of this. Trading connections can easily turn into borrowing and lending connections.

The countries which have borrowed most from abroad for development purposes are thus those which have at some stage had a colonial status, have been developed by European immigrants, or have traded heavily with the highly developed countries—or have satisfied all of these conditions. Australia, Canada, Chile, the Netherlands Indies, Mexico and Argentina all had foreign obligations in 1938 which amounted to more than a year of their income —and therefore to perhaps a third or more of their total capital. At an earlier date these proportions would probably have been higher for some of the countries mentioned. India, China, and Brazil had also been among the heavy foreign borrowers, though their external debts never became nearly so large in relation to their incomes (or probably, to their capital) as did those of the countries in the first group. The United States itself, in spite of its high rate of internal saving, was a heavy foreign borrower in the earlier part of its development, with a net foreign indebtedness which, in the eighteen-nineties perhaps reached 4 or 5 per cent. of its already very large capital.

The reasons for most of this borrowing have been reinforced by the second consideration mentioned earlier—the need for a developing country for foreign exchange to buy imports. In a sense, this is the same thing as the greater facility of borrowing externally as compared with internally. In so far as the difficulty and expense of internal borrowing arise from the low level of internal saving in relation to the investment which is desired, it will not be easy to get internally the real resources corresponding to this level of investment, either. If the people of the country insist on consuming all but, say, 5 per cent. of their output, it will not be easy to muster labour and other resources amounting to 10 per cent. of the economy's productive power for investment purposes, and the natural result of trying will be to create demand for net imports, either of things wanted for the investment programme, or of things to satisfy consumers' wants—the investment programme having drawn some internal resources away from the business of satisfying these wants. The result, namely demand for net imports, is much the same if the investment programme, unable to draw resources away from satisfying consumers' wants, takes them away from providing goods for export. The result may be similar in some degree even if the economy has (like many undeveloped economies) a substantial reserve of underemployed labour and other productive resources to draw upon. In this case it will be possible for the government, at least, to finance some investment expenditure by creating new money without any serious inflationary consequences. But the increased income which results, unless it can be skimmed off by higher taxation or diverted into bigger private savings, will still result in higher demand for imports. Some of the extra production must be diverted into export markets if this is not to result in foreign borrowing, and such a diversion may demand special efforts in marketing and other fields of activity.

But even if extra savings are forthcoming to match a programme of increased investment, without any considerable rise in consumption, it may still be true that the demand for imports is increased; the nature of the investment undertaken often requires heavy imports of capital goods, which the economy in question has not yet the equipment or the skills to produce for itself. It is not always easy, or even practicable, to expand exports to match this enlarged demand for imports; hence some of the pressure to finance part of investment by external borrowing, especially when the economy is in an early stage of development.

Borrowing from abroad therefore plays in most cases a very important, though rarely the major, part in financing economic growth, particularly in its early stages. It is, moreover, a very sensible process on general grounds. Development demands that people somewhere should refrain from spending part of their incomes, thus allowing part of the world's productive resources to be used for the accumulation of capital goods. The people who can best afford to do this are generally those who live in countries of high average income; on the other hand the countries where development is likely to alleviate suffering and promote welfare to the greatest extent are those where average incomes are low. There is a strong general case for the rich countries lending to the poor ones.

Unfortunately, this is not always easily arranged. As we have seen, rather special circumstances have usually had to exist before a really backward economy could borrow on a large scale from abroad. Profits are usually largest and interest payments to foreign lenders most certain not from the least developed countries, but from those which have overcome at least the initial barriers to development—have acquired efficient governments, interested in development, or private enterprises of considerable size and wealth, or both; and are expanding fast. Indeed, the largest and safest profits of all may come not from countries which are poor because there is little capital in them in proportion to their population, but from those (like Canada) which are already rich because they have plenty of natural resources and plenty of capital goods of kinds other than those which they are now hoping to acquire. The conventional picture of the rewards to further investment in an economy declining with every increase in the amount of investment already made in it, because the most lucrative opportunities are exploited first, may be seriously misleading. In practice, new discoveries of techniques or natural resources, and new expansions of markets are nearly always happening. It is more profitable to exploit a discovery of coal or oil in a country with good roads and railways and a growing industry than in one which is without these things. The undeveloped country often does not present good investment opportunities in any one line of economic activity unless it can be assumed that a good many other lines will be developed simultaneously—hence a great deal of the case for comprehensive development planning, which, in turn, is possible only in favourable social and political conditions.

It is not surprising, therefore, that lending from rich countries to poor ones has not happened on as large a scale, or as uniformly, as the general presumption in its favour would lead one to hope. There have, moreover, been strong barriers to it in the form of resentment at control of industry by foreigners, or at indebtedness to them. The great depression of the nineteen-thirties finally caused such a loss to international lenders through default on the interest due to them, and absence of profits, that private international lending sank to a low level from which it has only very partially recovered since. Public lending, through the Export-Import Bank established by the United States Government in the later nineteen-thirties, and more recently through the International Bank for Reconstruction and Development have become important, but have not served, even in the period of great economic expansion since 1950, to restore international lending to the place which it occupied in the generation before 1914, or in the nineteen-twenties. In its hey-day it constituted at least 5 per cent., and at times probably much more, of total net investment in the world; in recent years it has probably not risen to 2 per cent. of the world total.

United States aid to other countries has since the war been much greater than total international lending—a fact which has perhaps encouraged the quite widely held view that gifts or loans undertaken on a non-commercial basis, rather than loans on ordinary commercial terms, are what we must in future rely upon to make the resources of the rich countries available for the development of the poor ones. A Special United Nations Fund for Economic Development has, indeed, been advocated for this purpose, but so far without practical effect, as we shall note in Chapter 12.

We have now looked very briefly at the main economic factors which govern the growth of economies. Behind them lie the political, social, and religious conditions which determine the attitudes of the dominant people in an economy towards its development and their power to influence it—conditions which it is not within the scope of this book to examine. In the more strictly economic field, the twin agents of growth are, as we have seen, knowledge and capital. Both of them require for their acquisition some sacrifice of immediate enjoyment or immediate ease, or (what for a large community is usually practicable only on a limited scale), some borrowing from other economies. It is only occasionally in human history that the decision to make (or impose) this sacrifice, and to how large an extent, has been consciously taken by any ruler or ruling body. It is only very recently that electorates in democratic countries, in particular, have been faced with it, and it is safe to say that most of them still have not been presented with it in clear terms, or come to understand it. The decision to make sacrifices for posterity in war is recognized, and publicized, as one of the most crucial of all communal decisions; the corresponding issue in conditions of peace is rarely even formulated. This may be thought surprising, but if the reader accepts it as true, he will perhaps be less surprised that the branch of economics sketched in this chapter is not more highly developed.

H

CHAPTER 8

The Balance of Occupations

Farm Population and Productivity

ONE of the most striking differences between economies consists in the very wide variations in the proportions of their inhabitants with particular kinds of occupation. For the world as a whole, agriculture (in the broad sense of any sort of farming) is by far the most widely followed class of economic activity; about three-fifths of the world's families live on farms. This proportion varies geographically, however, from three-quarters or more in China, much of the Middle East, the Caribbean countries, and some of eastern Europe to about a quarter in much of western Europe, about an eighth in the United States, and as little as a twentieth in the United Kingdom. The proportions of population in the other occupations vary to corresponding extents.

The variation in the proportion of a population which we find engaged in agriculture (or any other class of production) is partly due, of course, to the fact that some countries are quite highly specialized. The low proportion in farming in the United Kingdom, for instance, is partly connected with the fact that we do not feed ourselves—we produce only rather less than half of the food we eat, and import the rest in exchange for (mainly) manufactured goods. Similarly, in countries like Canada, Australia and Denmark, the proportions in agriculture, although not by any means among the highest in the world, are as large as they are partly because those countries produce a great deal more agricultural produce than they use, and export the surplus in exchange for (mainly) manufactured goods and raw materials in which they therefore do not have to be self-sufficient. The reasons for, and the extent of, this kind of specialization by economies as a whole will have to be discussed in a future chapter. For the present, it is sufficient to note that it explains some of the occupational differences between different countries, but by no means the greater part of it. If the United Kingdom had a smaller population so that it could grow all of its own food, it would still have no more than a tenth of its population on farms. The proportion on farms in, say, China, which does not export agricultural products on a significant scale in relation to its production, is as we have seen, six or seven times as great as this.

The largest single reason for this wide variety in the ratios of farm population to total population is one which has already been discussed in Chapter 4—namely, the enormous range of difference between agricultural outputs per man on farms in different countries. It is not very hard to see that, if a farming family can produce enough to feed itself and, say, ten other families to the extent to which they can afford to be fed, then only one in eleven of the families in the country will be needed on farms to provide all the food demanded—foreign trade apart. Something like this is the situation in Australia, New Zealand, and much of North America, as we have seen. On the other hand, where a farm family can do little more than feed itself at subsistence level, nearly every family has to farm; the economy simply has not much left over for producing anything else after it has satisfied its minimum need for food.

Income and Diet

There is, of course, more in it than that; the amount and kind of food and other agricultural products consumed by a representative family also varies a great deal from one country to another, and that, too, has something to do with the proportion of the population which is required to produce the food in question. In fact, the countries with the highest proportions of their populations on farms tend to have poorer diets than those where the proportion is small; otherwise the contrasts between the occupational structures of different kinds of country would be even sharper than they are. This tendency is in accordance with what has been noted in Chapter 4 about productivity and general standards of living. The countries where farming is least productive, and where it therefore takes a lot of farmers to produce a given amount of food, are generally the poor countries. They are poor partly because farming is unproductive in relation to the number of people engaged in it, and partly because the same is true in such countries of other activities, such as manufacturing industry; otherwise, as we have seen, people would have moved out of farming into those other, more productive, activities. And so, because the production of most kinds of goods per person engaged in it is small in these countries, the standard of living, and the diet which people can afford, are both poor.

If the amounts of food consumed differed sufficiently between people at different levels of real income, that would, naturally, prevent differences in agricultural productivity from being adequate to explain differences in the proportions of the population engaged in farming. If, for instance, the populations of countries always spent half their incomes on food, whether their average incomes were high or low, we might expect that the proportions of the population engaged directly or indirectly in producing food would not, in any country, be very different from a half. We should certainly not get the enormous variation in this proportion which this chapter began by noting. In fact, however, food consumption per head, though it differs from country to country, does not vary nearly as much as agricultural productivity. Sometimes it is said that this is so because peoples' stomachs are all of much the same size; but that, though no doubt a relevant fact, is not an adequate explanation. There is a sense in which what people put into their stomachs does not vary very much from one country to another. If we measure food simply by its calorific value—its energy-producing power—we find (as we noted in Chapter 1) that the average diet in the richest countries, such as the United States, is only 30 per cent. or so greater than that in the poorest, such as India or China. But qualitatively these diets are very different, and the differences of quality have important economic consequences. The Chinese diet, for instance, consists very largely of rice and other vegetable foods with relatively little meat or dairy produce. The American or British diet, on the other hand, consists much more largely of meat and dairy products. Now, to get rice, you only have to grow it, but to get meat or milk you have first to grow crops (of grain, roots or grass) and then to feed them to animals. The calories that emerge finally from the milk or butter or meat are only a fraction—from a third to a tenth—of those originally fed to the animals. The result of this fact, along with the qualitative difference between the Chinese and American diets, is that some three times as much in the way of crops (measured by calorific value) has to be grown to feed an American as a Chinese at their present average standards, not to mention the extra labour which is involved in tending and milking or killing animals and processing the products, as compared with simply preparing a vegetable food like rice for human consumption. The diets of the richer communities therefore cost several times as much in resources as the diets of the poorer, despite the relatively small difference in their final calorific values. But the fact still remains that this difference is much smaller than the ten or twenty-fold difference which we noted in Chapter 4 between the amounts produced per head by agricultural populations in the productive (rich) and the unproductive (poor) countries. And it is the discrepancy between the productivity differences and the consumption differences that accounts for the variation in the proportion of the population engaged in producing food.

Another way of saying very nearly the same thing is to point out that the proportions of their incomes which communities spend on food are smaller in the rich communities than the poor ones. The proportion of the total income of the community which was spent on food (valuing all goods and services bought at American prices, so as to eliminate trouble due to the various classes of things having different relative prices in different countries) seems to have been in the year 1950, less than a fifth in the United States, just under a quarter in the United Kingdom, a little more in France and western Germany, and nearly a third in Italy. Whereas American use of goods and services as a whole per head of the population was between three and five times as large as Italian (we get different results, of course, according to whether we value everything at American or Italian prices), American average expenditure per head on food was only somewhere about twice as great as Italian. For poorer countries still, such as China and India, the proportion of the total income devoted to food is as much as two-thirds or three-quarters. Although their average real income per head is only a third or half that of Italy, the amount of it which is devoted to getting food is not very much less—indeed, it could not be; we are getting down towards the minimum food supply on which a population can subsist. The poorest communities can afford little more than their food, and not much of that; as we go to richer and richer communities we find that the average expenditure per head on food increases less than half as fast—proportionately—as average income.

The same thing can be seen by looking at the families with different levels of income within any community. Expenditure on food goes up, of course, with income, but not so fast, proportionately. A recent investigation in the United Kingdom shows that the percentage by which food expenditure changes is only a third or a quarter of the percentage by which income changes as we go from poorer families to richer ones, or the reverse; other investigations, both here and in other countries yield varying results, but none of them suggest that food expenditures rise in anything like a proportionate relation to income. For communities and for families it is true that the wealthy devote a small proportion of their resources to getting food, the poor a large one. A poor community, unless it relies heavily upon external trade, is bound to be largely agricultural; a rich one, unless it relies heavily upon external trade, cannot be so. Indeed, of the highly productive countries, even those which specialize to a considerable extent upon agriculture and export a good part of their agricultural output, such as Canada, Australia, New Zealand, and Denmark, have only about a quarter of their populations on farms. The 'flight from the land' which has given so much pain to observers in many countries is mostly an inevitable accompaniment of increasing productivity and rising standards of living.

Income and the Non-Agricultural Occupations

The proportions of the population engaged in other occupations in some cases, vary very markedly with the level of income of the community, and in other cases do not. There is not much variation with income in the proportion of the population to be found in, for instance, building or transport. Each of these classes of occupation accounts for perhaps something like 5 per cent. of the active population of the world, with variations from country to country which depend mostly upon geographical circumstances. One of the very striking contrasts in regard to transport is that between India, where it occupies only 2 or 3 per cent. of the population, and China, where it occupies something like 8 per cent.—a remarkable instance of the labour-saving power of India's relatively good communications. That the still better communications systems of more highly developed countries do not in general employ smaller proportions of the population than those of the less developed shows, of course, that dependence upon transport is one of the marks of an advanced economy. Very broadly speaking, the superior efficiency of labour working with the advanced transport equipment of the highly developed countries is matched by the greater demand for their services. In much the same way, the superior efficiency of labour in building and construction work in advanced countries seems just about to be matched by the greater demand for its products there— though that demand probably depends as much upon the rate at which the economy is growing as upon the standard of living which it has reached.

On the other hand, there are the occupations which employ increasing proportions of the population as we move to richer communities. Manufacturing industry is, on the whole one of these, but not, perhaps, to the extent that one might think. The proportion varies from less than 10 per cent. of the total occupied population in India, China, and some other very poor countries to between 35 and 40 per cent. in the most highly industrialized countries, such as the United Kingdom, Belgium, and Germany. These proportions depend, directly, upon two things—first the extent to which the country in question is a specialized manufacturing country, which exports more manufactures than it imports, or on the other hand, a net importer of manufactured products, and secondly, the extent to which the people who live in it choose to spend their incomes on manufactures. The importance of the first of these—specialization —is very considerable in, for instance, the United Kingdom. In recent years, this country has exported about 30 per cent. of the products of its manufacturing industry. Against this, however, we have to set off the manufactures which it imported, including the element of manufacture embodied in the country's imports of foodstuffs and raw (or semi-manufactured) materials. After allowing for these we can say that, if the United Kingdom had been able to produce at home all the goods and services it used, and had accordingly not had to export anything, the proportion of the occupied population we should have had to employ in manufacturing would have been only 28 or 30 per cent. instead of the actual 37. But this is still somewhat higher that the corresponding proportion in the United States, which is, of course, also a net exporter of manufactures, though only on a small scale in relation to its huge output of them. In fact, the proportion of its population which is required to work in manfacturing industry to supply it with manufactured goods increases from the very poor to the fairly poor countries, but does not increase further as we move from them to the rich.

What proportions of their income communities choose to spend upon manufactured goods is a matter on which we have, in general, only rather scrappy information. Mr Clark has done an elaborate calculation for a number of countries, but the methods he was obliged to adopt are rather precarious. On the whole, the evidence suggests that these proportions agree pretty well with the fractions of the occupied populations which are engaged in manufacture, if we make proper allowance for the extents to which there are net imports or exports of the products of manufacturing industry. Once again, the striking thing is that, apart from very poor countries like India where it is low, the proportion does not vary much, and, more particularly, does not change in a regular way with standard of living. It is no higher for the United States than for many countries with much lower standards of living.

There is, nevertheless, a sense in which communities increase their purchases of manufactures more than in proportion to the increase in their average incomes per head. This fact can be illustrated by statistics for the United States, the United Kingdom, and Italy, contained in a very careful study by the Organization for

European Economic Co-operation. In all three of the countries in question, clothing, household goods, transport equipment (bought by consumers), and producers' durable equipment together accounted in 1950 for just about a quarter of the total national expenditure. If, however, all goods and services bought in all three countries are valued at American prices, the ratio of the purchases of these classes of manufactured goods to total purchases falls to less than a sixth in the United Kingdom and to about a ninth in Italy. This simply means, of course, that manufactures are much cheaper relatively to goods and services in general in the United States than in the United Kingdom, and relatively cheaper here than in Italy. It is a point to which attention was drawn in Chapter 4; because American productivity is most superior to Italian in manufacturing industry, manufactured goods are cheaper in relation to other kinds of goods and services in America than in Italy. This relative cheapness of manufactured goods is no doubt in part responsible for the fact that Americans consume more of them, in proportion to their consumption of goods and services as a whole, than Italians do. Whereas the available quantity of goods and services per head (valued at American prices) is a little over three times as great in America as in Italy, the American consumption of the classes of manufactured goods mentioned above is about eight times as great as the Italian. But this proportionately greater consumption of manufactured goods in the richer country is probably a result even more of the high average incomes than of the relative cheapness of the goods in question.

Manufactures, then, are among the things of which communities increase their consumption more than in proportion to their income, but, except among the poorer countries, the increasing demand is balanced by the increasing efficiency of production, so that the percentage of the total labour force in manufacturing stays constant, or even declines a little (apart from the effects of specialization and trade) as we move from the fairly poor up to the richest economies. The occupations which absorb markedly higher proportions of the working force as income increases are, naturally, those for whose products demand increases sharply with income, provided that efficiency of labour in them is not too markedly superior in the more advanced economies, and provided, too, that if their products are dear in relation to other things in the richer countries, this does not choke demand off too much. Generally, these conditions seem to be fulfilled for the group of occupations connected with wholesale and retail distribution, finance, and insurance. The productiveness of highly productive economies depends largely upon specialization by individual producers, firms, and whole districts, which creates the demand for commercial and financial services to bind the economy together. And, so far, the labour engaged in these occupations in the productive economies is not superior in efficiency to that in the less productive countries in the same degree in which this is true of the labour in manufacturing industry, or even of the labour of the economy as a whole. The proportion of the occupied population in these activities therefore increases from 5 per cent. or less in the poorest economies to something like 15 or 20 per cent. in the richest.

Another group of which much the same is true is that which provides professional services of various kinds—medical, legal, educational—and entertainment. The proportion of the occupied population in this seems to increase in a fairly regular way from 1 or 2 per cent. in the poorest economies to 6 or 8 in the richest. On the other hand, there are some occupations which fulfil some, but not all, of the conditions mentioned in the last paragraph as conducive to their taking a high proportion of the manpower of wealthy economies. Private domestic service is one of these. There is undoubtedly a tendency for the proportion of income spent on these services to increase sharply with the incomes of the spending families within any economy. Moreover, in highly productive economies the provision of domestic service is not likely to be as efficient, in proportion to manufacturing and other kinds of production, as it is where these other industries are unproductive. For this very reason, however, domestic service, like most kinds of personal service, is relatively dear more or less in proportion to the productiveness, or standard of living, of the economy. Moreover, where it is dear, it is possible to find substitutes for it in the shape of labour-saving devices, more convenient houses, and tinned food. In the five countries—the United States, the United Kingdom, France, Western Germany, and Italy—for which careful calculations have been made, the proportions of the national income spent on domestic service (if all goods and services are valued, for uniformity, at American prices), stand clearly in the reverse order of standards of living, rising from less than 1 per cent. in the United States to nearly 3 per cent. in Italy. The tendency is to buy less domestic service, in proportion to real income per head, as real income per head goes up. But since, at local prices, domestic service is cheaper in relation to goods and services in general the poorer the country is, the proportion of actual income, valued at local prices, which is spent on this service turns out to be much the same in all five countries, and this may well have been roughly true of the proportions of the occupied populations engaged in it. The distribution of income between families has, however, a great deal to do with the demand for domestic service. The ability of one person to pay for the services of another out of his income clearly depends upon the difference of income between the employer and the employed. Certainly, the great decline in private domestic service in the United Kingdom (and probably other countries too) from perhaps 10 per cent. of the occupied population in 1841 to between 3 and 4 per cent. now is likely to owe at least as much to the equalizing effects of taxation as to the improvement in the average standard of living.

This chapter has sought to explain what it is that gives an economy its occupational structure. Apart from specialization and trade with other economies, to which we shall have to turn in the next chapter, we might say that it is the structure of demand—the way in which the community chooses to lay out its income. But this is itself shaped by many factors, of which we can clearly distinguish three; the general standard of living which determines how much has to be spent on necessities (especially food) and how much is left over for luxuries; the relative prices of different kinds of goods and services; and, as we saw from the instance of private domestic service, in some cases the way in which income is distributed. Of these three main factors, moreover, the first (the general standard of living) has already been seen to be connected with the average level of physical productivity, and the second (relative prices) with the relative productivities of labour and other resources in different kinds of production. This is as far as we can go for the time being.

CHAPTER 9

The Roots of Specialization

THE fact that most economies are in some degree specialized in their activity, that they produce more of some goods and services than they use and exchange the surplus with other economies for things of which they produce less than they use, has had to be noted several times in the foregoing chapters, but has so far been pushed aside to avoid complicating the discussion. Now it must be faced. Specialization, or division of labour, among its constituent parts, is what binds an economy together, making it the complicated organism which economists try to understand. Division of labour among the various national or regional economies of the world is, similarly, what makes it meaningful to speak of a 'world economy' with peculiar and complicated problems of its own.

Degrees of Self-Sufficiency
In fact, no important economy, except the whole world economy, is really quite self-contained, and what areas we choose to select for study as separate economies within the world economy, treating their internal structures and their external relations separately, is largely a matter of political and statistical convenience. That it is useful to study any national or regional economies as separate entities, putting in their relations with the rest of the world as a kind of after-thought, depends, indeed, upon two circumstances. The first is that some regional economies do, in fact, have relatively little to do with the rest of the world. The Soviet Union, for instance, produces all but 2 or 3 per cent. of the goods and services which it uses; the United States all but 4 or 5 per cent. The degree in which, by this simple test, economies are independent of the rest of the world tends to be greater the bigger the economy we are talking about; bigness makes for variety of resources. Much further down the scale we come to the United Kingdom which, by this test, is only about three-quarters self-sufficient (a low degree of self-sufficiency for an economy which, judged by its total production, is still one of the big ones, though much smaller than the U.S.A. or the U.S.S.R.). France, Western Germany, and Italy, all seem to be rather more than four-fifths self-sufficient; Sweden, Switzerland,

Canada and Japan show about the same degree of self-sufficiency as the United Kingdom. Small, wealthy countries like Norway, Belgium, Denmark, and New Zealand tend to be about two-thirds self-sufficient, or in some cases a little less. The least self-sufficient, of the politically separate territories are certain of the producers of agricultural products, fish or minerals—Venezuela, Malaya, and Iceland—where more (sometimes much more) than half the goods and services used are imported. This is a very high degree of 'openness', probably comparable with that which would be found (if the calculation could be made) for the economies of large cities within highly developed countries. The proportion of the total expenditure of residents in such cities which is paid for the provision within them of shopkeepers' and distributors' services, for house-room, on wages and salaries of local transport workers, caterers, and professional men and on the production of manufactured goods which are locally consumed (even assuming that by far the greater part of them is not), is likely to be between 40 and 50 per cent. In this sense, Leeds or Pittsburg may well be more self-sufficient than Northern Rhodesia, which was until recently a politically separate territory.

It must not be supposed, however, that this sense of the term 'self-sufficiency'—the proportion of the goods and services used in a community which originate within it—is the only, or even the most important one. In particular, it is only very loosely connected with the extent to which the community concerned is independent of contact with the outside world. The things imported, even though only a small proportion by value of the things used, may be essential for the production of a very large part of them. Of self-sufficiency in this perhaps more obvious sense there is no easy quantitative measure.

Large-scale Production and Local Specialization
Broadly speaking, territorial specialization springs from two roots; the fact that many kinds of production cannot be so efficiently undertaken on a small scale as on a larger scale, and the fact that many facilities for production are unevenly distributed over the world and are difficult or impossible to move about. In Chapter 4, some reference has already been made to the reasons for the efficiency of factory production, which mostly resolve themselves into the substitution of machinery for human work and the organization of the latter into team-work, so that the amount of time spent in teaching people their jobs and in their changing from one job to another is minimized, and so that work becomes

sufficiently repetitive and rhythmic to impose the minimum of
strain. It is plain that factory organization to these ends involves
specialization by the people concerned. It is by having each worker
specialize upon one relatively simple operation that the ratio of the
time spent in learning the job or getting ready for it to the time
spent doing it is reduced. Moreover, the multiplication of the kinds
of machinery which goes with highly organized factory production
means multiplication also of the kinds of expert—at all levels
from the designer to the maintenance man—and the larger scale of
organization itself demands all kinds of specialized experts on the
various aspects of management. But what is more to the present
point than the increase of specialization by individual people, which
factory production brings about, is the increase in specialization
by districts.

If production of a particular commodity is most efficient when the
unit—the factory—is one with a large output, then it's not efficient
to have a factory in every village or every small town, or even, in
extreme cases, in every country; it will be most economical for
production to be concentrated in a few plants. The extent to which
large-scale production is more efficient than small-scale varies
enormously from one industry to another, and there are not many
cases where it is possible to measure its superiority satisfactorily.
Moreover, the statistics of most countries are designed to conceal
rather than to reveal information about individual firms or plants,
so that, in the industries where most of the production within a
country comes from a few large plants, the facts are not easy to
come by. Nevertheless, a few facts can be quoted to illustrate the
importance, in some industries, of the minimum unit of efficient
production being large.

Take, for instance, the iron and steel industry. The modern large
blast furnace, which has considerable economic advantages on
account of its size, produces enough pig-iron for an advanced
community of something like a million people; it is usual to place
a number of such furnaces together in a single plant connected with
facilities producing enough steel for a community of at least two or
three million; if the steel is to be rolled by the efficient continuous
process into sheet and strip, a single plant may well be sufficient to
supply enough of these commodities for a community of twenty
million. A rolling plant for producing specialities such as broad
beams may serve an even bigger population.

The motor industry affords another example. It seems, on balance,
to be the case that the efficiency of production of motor vehicles can
be increased as the scale of manufacture of the model in question

is increased up to, at any rate, an output of about 100,000 a year. This is a large output—equal to about a fifth of the sales of cars within the United Kingdom in 1955. This means that (allowing for the demand for a variety of different models) any market much smaller than that of the United Kingdom would be too small to allow anything like the full economies of large-scale production to be realized; indeed, the most popular American models probably gain a good deal in cheapness from being produced on several times the scale just mentioned. Other transport equipment tends also to be produced on a big scale in relation to the total demand. With ships, aircraft, and locomotives, this is partly because the machines themselves are big in relation to the total demand for them, so that the number of new ones required each year is not very large; in the United Kingdom a few hundred locomotives and ships and a few score of non-military aircraft, even including the considerable proportion of these vehicles which are destined for export. About three-quarters of the work done on locomotives in the the United Kingdom (measured by value) is done in thirty-eight factories, three-quarters of that on aircraft in twenty-three factories, and more than half the shipbuilding in thirty-six yards. These figures probably understate the extent to which the final assembly of the vehicles takes place in a few establishments. Of all the perhaps 3,000 aircraft flying on scheduled services in the world (apart from the U.S.S.R.) in 1956, well over half are the products of the single firm of Douglas; the fleets of the world's fourteen largest airlines (comprising about half the above-mentioned total of air liners) consist overwhelmingly of a dozen types, assembled in probably about a dozen factories. The immense cost of developing a modern airliner, and the small number which the world requires even of the more successful types, make it inevitable that the world's demand for commercial air transport will continue to be satisfied by a very small number of aircraft factories in the future. Behind the assembly plants, whether for ships, motor cars, or aircraft, there stand, of course, an immense number of factories producing components. Many of these however, are highly specialized and concentrated; the number of factories in the world producing sparking-plugs, for instance, must be very small.

In other fields, besides transport equipment, the same principles also apply. In some cases the demand of a very large community for a particular product can be satisfied by one efficient machine of large capacity (as with the machine which can cut enough match-sticks for a population of five to ten million, that which can blow the bulbs for enough electric lamps to supply half the United Kingdom, or that which can produce enough glass containers for a population of a million). In some, the cost of developing the product is so large and the demand for it so limited (as with electronic computors and gas turbines) that the number of producing establishments is bound to be small. Sometimes it is a whole set of productive equipment (like an assembly line for motor cars, radio sets, or refrigerators) that constitutes the large, indivisible unit of efficient production. Sometimes it is the possibility of handling materials in large bulk by automatic methods with little more staff than is required to handle them in much smaller bulk, as in oil refining, where one modern unit can produce a third of the motor spirit required by the United Kingdom. Sometimes the possibility of increased thermal efficiency in a large heat engine is important, as in the generating sets of 200,000 Kw. capacity now being developed for the British Electricity Authority (a single set of this size would supply a city the size of Leeds). The large scale of economic plants for providing nuclear power depends, it would seem, on the fact that the control mechanisms and chemical processing plants required in connection with them do not increase in cost nearly as fast as they increase in capacity.

Altogether, therefore, there is a considerable part of the manufactured output of an advanced economy—perhaps something between one- and two-fifths—in which the community served by a single productive unit of the highest efficiency has a population reckoned in hundreds of thousands, and in some cases in millions. Even, therefore, if all the resources required for any kind of production were spread evenly throughout an area, we should not find all the kinds of production carried out in every part of the area; some of them would have to be localized simply because they can be carried out efficiently only on a large scale. This fact alone is responsible for a good deal of the local specialization within a country; it is less likely to be responsible, by itself, for international division of labour, but there are instances in which it is important on this larger scale also. A country with the population and income of New Zealand or Norway, or even one with a population and income of Denmark or Switzerland, could not produce rolled steel products, motor cars, large aircraft, electric light bulbs, or oil refinery products with the highest efficiency for its own market alone even with every natural advantage. It would therefore have a strong tendency either to import such products or, if it produced them, to do so on a large scale for export. Even with countries which provide considerably bigger internal markets—Belgium, the Netherlands, Australia—these tendencies are still of some importance.

The Distribution of Resources

The whole picture is, however, greatly complicated by the fact that productive resources are very far from being evenly distributed; it is on this ground that local and national specialization have traditionally been mainly explained. The difficulties of measuring resources are so great that it is hardly worth while, in this connection, to quote statistics, even for purposes of illustration. The distribution of agricultural land, for instance, varies enormously according to whether (as in an estimate made for the Food and Agriculture Organization) one considers only the 7 per cent. of the earth's land surface described as 'suitable for agriculture', or whether one follows Mr Clark in taking the whole land areas and 'weighting' each part of it by a factor intended to reflect its climatic suitability—though one which probably makes insufficient allowance for variations in soil quality. All estimates, however, agree in showing the poverty of Asia in land; with more than half the world's population it has, by any reasonable criterion, only something like a fifth of the world's natural agricultural resources. Europe also, in spite of some conflict of evidence, seems on balance to have less than its 'share' of natural agricultural producing-power in proportion to its population. At the other extreme, Oceania clearly has resources of this kind in great abundance in relation to population, and the Americas and Africa, though again there is a great difference in the result according to the method of estimation, are quite well off.

With sources of power matters are no easier. Looking at the known deposits of coal and oil, and sources of inland water-power, one sees that Europe seems to be, on a general view, the poorest of the continental areas in relation to population. North America is, on the other hand, decidedly the richest, and the Soviet Union is also well endowed. Africa's poverty (so far as is known) in oil and coal are compensated for by her enormous reserves of water-power, and South America's lack of coal by her water-power and oil. But it must be remembered that present knowledge even of the world's coal resources is very incomplete, and of the world's oil resources far more so. The distribution of total resources of either of these kinds may not be very much like the distribution of those deposits which are known at present. Even with water-power, where the potential resources are much better known, estimates of the kinds referred to here suffer from the great disadvantage—as do those relating to mineral fuels—that they do not reflect the enormous differences in cost and difficulty of use between one source and another. Moreover, in speaking of sources of power, one has to remember the nuclear fuels, sources of which are also only very partially explored.

It is clear, however, that if we look at even the most highly generalized picture of the world's basic resources, we see that population, agricultural land, and power are very far from being similarly distributed. The more detailed—the less generalized—we make the picture, the greater the discrepancies of distribution become. Not only are the resources mentioned in many cases highly localized within the continental areas to which they belong—like oil in the middle East—but agricultural land suitable for particular crops, like sugar cane, or coffee, or grapes, or cotton, is obviously much more unevenly distributed over the world than agricultural land in general. When we come to mineral resources other than fuel, their localization is equally striking. Over four-fifths of the known deposits of copper ore in the world, for instance, are in the United States, Chile, and the African 'copper-belt'. It is perhaps easier to look at the matter from the other end, and to point out that, of twenty-seven principal minerals, the United States, even under the impulse of war, did not become self-sufficient in seventeen, and was unable to supply itself with seven of them from within the western hemisphere; that the U.S.S.R. at the same time was not self-sufficient in at least ten, while the United Kingdom was self-sufficient in only three and Japan in only about half a dozen.

The Use of Resources
What would one expect to be the effect of this uneven geographical distribution of resources on the distribution of economic activities? In part, it seems obvious; minerals, for instance, can be dug out of the earth only in the particular places where they occur, and food can be grown only where land is above a certain standard of suitability. But these restrictive conditions do not always go very far towards explaining what actually happens. Some minerals, it is true, occur only in rare and localized deposits, as we have noted, but many are much more widespread, and there can be few instances in which every known deposit of a mineral in the world is worked. In the same way, it is possible, technically, to grow nearly anything nearly anywhere with the assistance if need be of irrigation, glasshouses, fertilizers, and other aids. Adam Smith long ago pointed out that excellent grapes could, with such assistance, be grown in Scotland. It is not even the case that the most technically suitable land for a particular purpose, down to some particular standard of suitability, is used for that purpose all over the world. Land is used for growing grain in Greece or Italy which

I

is much less suitable for that purpose, by any technical standard, then much land which is used for rough pasture, or even not used at all, in Britain or the United States. Equally, much of the land which is used for building in one place would be better for some agricultural purpose than much of the land which is used for farming in other places. Two questions seem to arise from this: why does it happen? and: would it happen if the use of resources were sensibly planned?

The immediate reason why it happens is mainly that, in countries like Greece and Italy, people are willing to farm poor land for a small wage or income, whereas in Britain or the United States they are not. The reason for this, in turn, is one which has been mentioned before. In the United States, or Britain, there is plenty of scope for making better incomes elsewhere, either in growing grain on better land, or working in industry, where output per head is high, or doing some other job where, though the output per head may not be high in physical terms, the pay is high simply because there is a high *average* physical productivity in the economy as a whole. In countries like Italy or Greece, where the average physical productivity in the economy is much lower, this is not the case. The general level of income is low because the average level of physical productivity is low. Many people, therefore, cannot do better than farm poor land which yields only a poor income.

If we try to trace the causes further, it appears that the high average productivity of labour in the British or the American economy as compared with the Greek or the Italian can be accounted for by a greater abundance of some kind or kinds of resources, in relation to the number of people. This abundance might, in principle, be an abundance of land of superior quality to that which we began by considering, or an abundance of industrial equipment, or of industrial know-how and organizing ability. The essential point is that American or British land of a particular quality is not used, whereas Greek or Italian land of the same quality is, because Britain and the United States have abundant or superior resources of some other kinds in connection with which their available labour can be more productively engaged, while Greece and Italy have not.

When the reason for the use of a particular grade of resource in one part of the world but not in another is reduced to this form, it comes very near to being a statement about the 'reasonableness' of the arrangement. If a community were planning its own activities, it would probably think it sensible to allocate a man to a particular job only if he could add at least as much to the total product of the community in that job as in any other. (We can assume for the sake of this argument that the additional product he adds by his activity in the job is adequately measured by its market value; that is to say, by what buyers are prepared to pay for it.) Planners in Italy or Greece would think it worth allocating man-power to the working of poor land and mineral deposits which could be mined only with much labour, because there were not enough resources to make the labour more productive in another job. British or American planners would grudge labour to similarly (or even rather less) poor land or mineral deposits, because they could be worked only at the cost of denying it to jobs in which it could be more productive. The movement of labour, or for that matter other resources, to those uses where it can earn most is likely to happen—and is in fact seen to happen—in communities where such movements are free. If there is a reasonably close connection between what a man can earn in a job and what he adds to the output of the community by doing it (a matter which was touched upon in Chapter 6), then this movement is also one which a central planning authority would approve, as tending to maximize the national output.

Broadly speaking, concentrating on the use of the resources that yield the biggest incomes means concentrating on those which are most unusually accessible, or of the most unusually high quality (judged by general, world, standards) in the particular district or area under discussion. It may be that it is an area where all kinds of natural resources are more available, in relation to the size of the population, or are of better quality, than in most other parts of the world. That would ensure that the people of that area have the prospect of being unusually well off; it does not guarantee that they will use all the kinds of resources with which they are so well provided. They will do best by using those with which, to repeat, they are *most* unusually well provided. In that way they will make the biggest income open to them (measured in money value), and will be able to use some of it to buy from other areas the goods which those areas produce, specializing according to the same principle. In this way it may come about, as we have seen, that some resources in which the area in question is richer than most (or even than any) other areas may go unused, because it is still more outstandingly well equipped with other resources, which it therefore pays it to concentrate upon developing.

In the same way, an area which is poorly provided with all kinds of natural resources in proportion to its population is at a disadvantage in comparison with others better provided, and may for that reason never be able to equal them in standard of living. It will do best by concentrating in some degree upon the use of the kind of resource in which it is least poor (by general world standards), even though that resource is poorer or harder to work than those of the same kind in more favoured places—where, as we have seen, they may not even be used.

The reader may still think there is something irrational in this, and so, in a sense, there is; but given that population and resources are distributed in the sort of way we have described, the rules which have just been given for getting the best possible standard of living in each area are unassailable. The irrationality lies in the distribution of population. People can, in principle, move about, and if it is correct to assume (as we have done) that they will change their jobs within their own district in order to better their incomes, is it reasonable to suppose that they will fail to move, for the same reason, from places which are relatively poor in all resources to places that are relatively rich? If they moved in this way sufficiently freely, they would, presumably, come near to wiping out the differences in standards of living between different parts of the world. In that case, it would be much less likely to happen that (say) land of a particular kind was worked in one country, but not in another. If it yielded enough to attract and hold labour in one country, similar land with a similar physical yield would be able to attract and hold labour in others. If in one country there were more plentiful resources of other kinds competing for the available labour, that would be offset by the greater supply of labour present to work with them. It would come much nearer to being true than it is now that all the best land for wheat-growing in the world, down to a uniform level of suitability, was used for wheat growing, all the most easily mined coal down to a uniform level of difficulty was being worked, and so on. This, presumably, is more like the way in which matters would be arranged by a world planning authority which wanted to get the best out of the world's resources, and was able to move people about as it wished in order to do it.

The Distribution of Population
Population, however, is immobile if one is thinking about only fairly short periods. Given time, the distribution of population can change very drastically either by migration or as a result of a faster rate of natural increase—a greater excess of births over deaths—in one region than in another. These two influences have combined to raise, for instance, the population of the Americas (north and south) from about 5 per cent. to over 13 per cent. of the world total in the last hundred years; it increased more than five-fold while world population as a whole doubled. At the other extreme, heavy emigration

coupled with a rate of natural increase which in the later part of the period was below the world average have almost halved the population of Ireland since the famine of 1846. It did not take the population of the United Kingdom much more than a century to change from living four-fifths in the country to living four-fifths in towns. In a decade or two, however, it is very rare indeed for the distribution of population to change very much; neither emigration nor immigration from or into any considerable region in a year often exceeds 1 or 2 per cent. of the number there at the beginning of the year, while natural increase cannot normally exceed 3 per cent. in a year and is considered rapid if it reaches half that rate.

Moreover, population changes are to a considerable degree independent of economic resources. It is true that, as was noted in Chapter 7 the biggest long-distance population movement of all, the emigration of some seventy million people from Europe to various overseas countries in last century and the early part of this, was very largely due to the opening up of the New World and the better livings that it promised as compared with the Old. The shorter-distance movement from the country into towns is also largely a movement of people to the places where new productive resources are, which can yield them higher incomes. It is also true that in some very poor countries the rate at which population could grow has been limited by the general power of production (which in such a poor community means mainly the power to produce or to buy food), so that population and other productive resources have had to keep in step. Nevertheless, the correspondence between the distribution and growth of population and the distribution and growth of other resources is only a loose one. The great migrations of the nineteenth century were checked in the twentieth largely because of their very tendency to spread population more evenly in relation to resources —which would have meant lowering the standards of living in the countries which were wealthy because of their high ratios of resources to people. Even where there are no definite political barriers to adjustment, as in the movement of people from country to town, there are other barriers of many kinds, of which unwillingness to change without very good reason is perhaps the greatest. Consequently, the adjustment of population to changes in resources nearly always lags behind those changes. That is probably the chief reason for the fact that, in most countries, average incomes of families in agriculture are much lower than those of families earning their living in manufacturing industry or commerce. The general increase in productivity and the accumulation of industrial and commercial capital have called for a change in the balance of occupations away from agriculture, as we saw in the last chapter; but because people are slow to move, labour is scarcer in industry and commerce than it is in agriculture so long as this process is going on—and consequently industrial and commercial wages are higher than agricultural.

Moreover, the differences between rates of natural increase in different countries, which are responsible for most of the large-scale changes in the distribution of population, are very far from being connected closely with differences in resources or income. Apart from the very poor countries where, as we have noted, food supply (and therefore productive power) limits population growth, the latter as often falls with an increase in wealth as it rises with it. The richest country—the United States—has at present rather a high rate of natural increase (about $1\frac{1}{2}$ per cent. a year), but the communities in the next richest group (western Europe, in particular) mostly have rates of increase not much above $\frac{1}{2}$ per cent. The fact seems to be that wealthy communities which are also in general the most highly urbanized and the most highly educated, tend to have rather small families. Birth rates are low, but death rates are also low, since the standards of feeding, clothing, housing and hygiene are relatively high. On the other hand, in countries where the standards of hygiene are low, death rates are high. Families are large (or, at any rate the birth rate is high)—the community would not survive otherwise, and even as it is, may achieve only a low rate of increase. If, in addition to low standards of hygiene there is low productive power, so that food and other necessities are inadequate, this is all the more so. The countries which have low standards of hygiene nowadays are nearly all poor, but by no means all poor countries have low standards of hygiene; in particular the control of diseases like cholera, malaria, and plague and the use of the new antibiotic drugs are becoming very widespread. Consequently, there are a good many countries now which retain the high birth rates which until recently did little more than offset their high death rates, but where the death rate has begun to fall—not because of any change in general economic resources or the general effectiveness with which they are used, but solely on account of improvement in the control of diseases, and public hygiene generally. Ceylon, Puerto Rico, and, in a less striking degree, India are examples of this. China may be about to follow their lead. These countries are experiencing or seem to be about to experience, very rapid rises in population which are not connected with abundance of resources, or with any increase in their productive power. On the face of it, this development seems likely to widen the difference between the distribution of population and the distribution of resources.

The disproportionate distribution of population in relation to natural resources, like the disproportionate distribution of the various kinds of natural resource in relation to each other, is therefore something that has to be taken for granted. We have seen that it creates certain presumptions about the way in which natural resources will be used, each area concentrating in some degree upon the development of the resources with which it is most outstandingly well, or least outstandingly badly, equipped. This is, in effect one way of stating the celebrated economic proposition known as the 'law of comparative advantage'. Before we can extract the full meaning out of this proposition, however, we have to take account of the further, very important, facts, that people and natural resources are not the only things upon which production immediately depends, and that, while natural resources (in the sense of land, mineral deposits, waterfalls and so on) are certainly immovable, this need not pin down the industries that use agricultural products, minerals, or power—since these are all, in varying degrees, transportable.

The Distribution of the Conditions of Progress

The requisites for production, apart from people and natural resources, are principally capital, skill, knowledge, a certain degree of political security, and a disposition to organize production and to take part in it. These also are very unevenly distributed about the world, by no means in proportion to population or any other kind of productive resources. For a particular year, or even for longer, their distribution has also to be taken as given, but it is alterable to a drastic extent over not very long periods of time by human action —more so, in general, than is the distribution of population itself.

We have seen in Chapter 7 that the rate of saving—this is to say, the rate at which an economy accumulates capital—varies over a wide range, from less (perhaps much less) than 5 per cent. of its income in the slowest cases to a fifth or a quarter of it in the fastest. If we take it that capital already in existence amounts to one or two years' income in countries of the kind that usually save least of their income, and three or four years' income in those which save faster, this means that the percentage rate at which capital grows can vary from 2 or 3 per cent. a year on the one hand (or perhaps less) to perhaps 7 or 8 per cent. on the other. We have seen, also, that the conditions which make for very rapid saving—for an industrial revolution, in fact—are rather special;

they consist in certain combinations of attitudes, institutions, governmental policies, and (in some degree) foreign trading and borrowing connections which are very far from existing everywhere, though, since the recipes are coming to be widely known, they are more likely to arise in any given country than used to be the case. They are also capable of arising with surprising rapidity. It is worth remembering that it took Germany only fifty years to move from the backwardness and muddle of the mid-nineteenth century to a position from which she challenged British industrial and commercial leadership, Russia less than thirty from the start of the first Five-Year Plan to the launching of the first sputniks. Both Japan and the Soviet Union probably quadrupled their capital in twenty years. It is because industrial revolutions are cumulative and rapid and the conditions for them do not exist everywhere, that we find the enormous differences in supplies of capital, knowledge, technical skill, and organizing power which limit the industries requiring most of these factors, for the time being, to particular parts of the world.

The Effects of Transport
Having looked at the manner and degree in which the main factors of production are localized, we must now consider briefly how the effect of this on the location of various kinds of economic activity is modified by the transportability, if not of the factors themselves, at least of some of their immediate derivatives. It has already been remarked—indeed, it is obvious—that some activities, like the cultivation of the land and the mining of minerals—are completely restricted to certain parts of the world by the facts of physical geography; though we have also seen that *which* of these resources are to be worked, and in what way, depends also on general economic circumstances or, basically, on the supply and quality of other factors of production. How far other activities are restricted depends, however, on the costs of moving raw materials and power from their places of origin and of taking products to their place of use.

Something has already been said in Chapter 4 about the relative efficiencies of different means of transport as load-carriers. In money terms, the average cost of moving goods on British Railways, making allowance for the cost of maintaining and eventually replacing the permanent way, and for the fact that, inevitably, trains are only partly full, seems to be something over 4d. a ton-mile. The cost of carriage in ocean steamers (other than tankers) making corresponding allowances, seems to be not much more than $\frac{1}{4}$d. a ton-mile. On British roads—making allowance for the cost of upkeep of the road itself—the cost seems to be anything up to twice as much as by rail. These are, of course, very broad averages, and the cost, like the actual charge, varies very much from one kind of freight to another. These figures give, nevertheless, some indication of the importance of distance in cost of production—provided that we know how much material has to be brought in to make the product with which we are concerned.

Quantities of material show an enormous variation from one industry to another. In iron smelting, for instance, it may be as high as 2,000 tons a year for every man employed, even if fuel is excluded. In oil refining it may be as great, or greater. Some of the agricultural processing industries—butter-making, sugar-refining, flour-milling, seed-crushing—are also 'heavy' in this sense; they require several hundred tons of materials a year for each employee. So, perhaps less surprisingly, do the cement and fertilizer industries. With the heaviest industries, the bringing in of the materials for one employee by rail—even at the cheapest rates, as charged for minerals— amounts to several pounds per year for each mile of average distance. With an average haul of a hundred miles, therefore, this transport bill alone might exceed the cost of all the labour used in processing the material when it arrives. Where the material can be brought in by sea, a haul of a thousand miles probably costs less than a rail haul of a hundred would cost; distance, nevertheless, still matters a great deal. For such industries, nearness to the sources of raw materials is clearly very important.

The cost of taking the product to market, however, obviously matters also. Most usually, it matters somewhat less than the cost of bringing in the raw materials, because the weight and bulk of the finished product is usually less—though the method of fixing railway rates according to 'what the traffic will bear' may tend to offset this difference. There are also exceptions—boxes and other containers are bulkier than the materials from which they are made, and therefore are nearly always manufactured near to the place where they are to be filled. Bread is heavier than the flour from which it is made; the added material (water) being available in any populated district, it therefore normally pays to bake near to the market rather than near to the flour-mill. Sometimes, too, the products have nearly the same weight and bulk as the materials—oil refinery products, for instance, are derived from crude oil with little less. Most 'heavy' industries, however, involve some loss of weight between the materials and the product, and the greater this loss, the more they are tied to the sources of their materials. If (as usually happens) these come from different places, the industry will be tied most closely to the source of the material which has the highest transport cost (per mile) for each ton of finished product. Nowadays, for instance, iron and steel plants which use low-grade ore are usually built near to the ore, or to ports to which it can be brought cheaply by water; formerly, where high-grade ore was used, and before modern methods had reduced the amount of coal used for each ton of steel, it was the cost of transporting the coal that predominated, and plants tended to be built on the coalfields, where many of them still remain.

For most industries, however, transport costs are much less than for the specially 'heavy' ones. Most of the branches of engineering, for instance (excluding structural engineering) use between ten and twenty-five tons of materials per year for each person occupied in them, and for the textile and clothing industries the amount is below (sometimes far below) the lower of these limits. The cost of carrying the materials, even over quite a long distance, is in all these cases fairly small in comparison with the industry's labour-bill, and inter-regional, or international, variations in the cost and efficiency of labour are therefore likely to be more important for them than variations in material prices which are due to transport costs—or variations in the cost of marketing the product which are due to the same cause.

Some industries are tied down to an appreciable extent by their power requirements. In manufacturing industry as a whole, fuel and purchased energy account for only a small proportion of total cost—usual about 3 or 4 per cent. For blast furnaces however, the proportion is as high as a quarter, for brickworks, cement-works and aluminium-smelting a fifth or more. In some branches of the chemical and fertilizer industries, it is higher still. In such cases, local differences in the price of power or fuel matter a great deal, though the possibility still exists, in most cases, that they may be outweighed by local differences in the price of some other factor of production.

Fuel and power vary in price from place to place of course, partly because costs of production differ from one place to another, partly because of costs of transporting them. Coal mining costs, for instance, vary enormously from one coalfield to another because of differences in thickness, regularity, and depth of seams, to say nothing of differences in the price of labour. Even within the United Kingdom they are more than twice as high in some areas as in others. So, for similar reasons, do costs of bringing crude petroleum out of the ground in various producing areas, and the costs of producing water-power on various sites where it is possible to do it. The tendency is for a source of energy in a particular district to be unused if fuel or power can be more cheaply brought in from outside. In the areas which could produce only at a high cost, therefore, or those which could not produce at all, power costs are higher than elsewhere by an amount which depends simply on the cost of bringing fuel or electricity in. The cost of coal is usually doubled by a rail haul of between two and four hundred miles, or by a sea voyage of between three and five thousand miles. In some parts of South America, some distance from the coast, coal might be sold in bulk at three times its cost at its point of origin at the pit-head in the United Kingdom or the United States. Crude oil is a good deal cheaper to move; ocean tankers carry it at less than a tenth of a penny per ton-mile, so that the cost of transport over the six thousand miles from the Persian Gulf to northern Europe is considerably less than the price of the oil at the beginning of its journey. Overland transport by pipe-line costs four or five times as much as this per ton-mile, but still only a fourth or a fifth of the cost by rail.

Transmission of electric power is a relatively short-range method of transporting energy. The cost per mile rises with the distance; greater distance requires higher voltage which in turn brings higher costs of transformation and insulation, besides introducing new technical difficulties and losses. So far, three hundred miles seems to be the furthest distance which it is worth transmitting power even from hydro-electric stations in which the costs of generation are very low. For shorter distances than this, when the electricity is generated from coal, it is sometimes hard to decide between bringing the coal to stations near the place where the power is to be used and transmitting the power from generating stations on the coalfield. The British Electricity Authority has recently decided that the latter is the more economical way of using the relatively cheap coal of the east midlands to supply London and the south and south-west of England; but the margin of advantage does not seem to have been very great.

Mechanical energy in manufacturing industry is now largely, and increasingly, derived from electricity, supplied either from large coal-fired generating stations (to which we now have to add generating stations in which nuclear reactors take the place of coal furnaces), or from water-turbines. The cost of upkeep and replacement of the plant for generating and distributing electricity (quite apart from the cost of transmitting it over long distances, which has already been mentioned) is very considerable, and, assuming that modern plant is used, varies relatively little from place to place. The wide differences in fuel costs which have been mentioned are therefore reflected in much smaller percentage differences in costs of electric power. It has been calculated that, at the prices of 1946, electricity from modern oil- or coal-fired plants would have cost much the same (0·4 to 0·6 of an American cent per unit) nearly anywhere in North America, Europe, South Africa, north-eastern India, or the more populous parts of the Soviet Union and Australia. The cost runs appreciably higher than this in most of South America and India, and, no doubt, in most of Africa and some of central Asia as well. At the highest it goes up to 0·8 to 1·0 cents a unit. On the other hand, the more easily-harnessed water-power sites bring the cost down locally to 0·1 to 0·3 cents a unit, as is shown by present experience in Norway, the Alps, the Dnieper, Tennessee and St Lawrence Valleys, and in Washington State and British Columbia. To these we shall no doubt have to add the areas of cheap water-power now being developed in the valleys of the Zambezi, Volta, Nile, and elsewhere. It seems, therefore, that the cost of power, in the form which it is mainly used by industry, does not vary very widely throughout the more populous parts of the world (with some exceptions in India), apart from rather limited areas of very cheap water-power. Nuclear energy is likely merely to cheapen power in places where it is now dearest (many of them at present thinly populated), and to prevent it from becoming dearer generally with the exhaustion of mineral fuels.

A General View of Localization
What, then, can be said about the localization of the various kinds of economic activity in the light of all these considerations? It has been noted that the tendency is for any area to specialize to some extent upon the kind of economic activity for which it is most outstandingly well equipped or least outstandingly badly equipped in comparison with other areas. This is the famous Law of Comparative Advantage (or as it is sometimes called, of Comparative Cost). The practical test of how outstandingly well (or badly) equipped an area is for providing a particular good or service lies in the prices at which it, and other areas, can provide that, and other, goods and services. The things which it can provide more cheaply, in relation to other goods and services, than other areas can, are the thing on which it is most likely to specialize—and on which it will best pay it to specialize.

For nearly forty years economists have been accustomed to taking this argument a stage further. The prices at which commodities can be provided are made up of the prices of the various factors of production which go to provide them, each duly multiplied by the amount of that factor which goes into a unit of the product. It follows, therefore, that the things which a particular area should be able to produce more cheaply than other areas, in relation to other things, are those which are made up to the greatest extent of the factors of production in which the area has a comparative advantage —those factors of production which are cheaper there, in relation to other factors, than is the case in other areas. An area where labour is cheaper in relation to the other factors than in other areas will be likely—and well advised—to specialize upon lines of production where a high proportion of the cost is attributable to labour. One where capital and power are cheaper in relation to other factors than they are elsewhere may be expected to specialize on products which demand relatively heavy use of capital and power.

This doctrine, however, must be interpreted carefully; its application to the modern world is complicated by several considerations, of which two may be mentioned here. The first of these is that it may be misleading to speak of products which demand relatively large amounts of labour or of capital, as if this were characteristic of them the world over. In the United States, the principal kinds of agricultural production are carried on with a higher ratio of capital equipment to man-hours of work than are most kinds of manufacture. In many other countries which produce at least some of the kinds of goods which figure in this comparison, the reverse is probably the case. A country where capital is dear in relation to labour and one where labour is dear in relation to capital may, therefore, both find that certain agricultural products are among the things which they can best export—the methods by which they are produced being widely different in the two places. (Egyptian and American cotton may be, or may be about to become, cases in point.)

The second point is the now familiar one that certain 'factors of production' are difficult or impossible to measure or to price in any precise way, and for that reason are apt to be overlooked in discussions of this kind. It comes as a shock to learn, for instance, that the manufactures which the United States exports most easily are, in general, those which demand (in the United States, at least), a relatively high ratio of labour to capital in their production, despite the fact that man-hours of labour are probably dearer in relation to capital in the United States than anywhere else. The explanation seems to be that American labour, when working in many factory industries, is rendered highly efficient by the existence of conditions (one might call them 'factors of production') which are not present to so great an extent elsewhere—good management, good technological education, good design of the product and the method of making it, as well as attitudes on the part of the workpeople themselves which make them well adapted to highly mechanized and rapidly developing methods of production. For most finished manufactured goods, the cost of labour, direct and indirect, is a very much larger part of the total cost of production than is the cost of the capital involved, which consists of interest on the capital directly and indirectly concerned in their production. The fact that for social, educational, and other reasons, Americans are good at factory production of highly manufactured goods (in relation to their efficiency in other kinds of production) can therefore outweigh the effect of the relative cheapness of capital, which in itself would tend to give them the comparative advantage in lines of production where the ratio of capital to labour cost is higher—mining, metal smelting, and perhaps even agriculture.

With these modifications to the general principle in mind, and remembering also the other points which have been made earlier in this chapter, we can reach some general conclusions. Whether a district specializes upon the extractive industries—agriculture and mining—depends primarily upon its endowment of agricultural or mineral resources (in a sense which includes their accessibility) considered in relation to its other factors of production. Wherever agricultural and mineral resources are scarce in relation to population, in particular, it is likely that, eventually, that population will be able to do best by specializing to some extent on manufacturing (as in Japan and the United Kingdom) though for the time being the social, political, and educational conditions may not be favourable to the building up of manufacturing industry, as was until recently the case in India and China, for instance.

But, in considering how well provided an area is with any particular resource, we have to take into account not only its internal source of supply, but also the ease with which supplies of it can be brought in—if they can be moved at all. Any place to which goods can be brought in bulk by water, for instance, can be regarded as fairly well supplied with all the main raw materials, fuels and foodstuffs; there will be differences between them according to distance from the source, but these differences will not, in general, be very great. Certainly they are small in comparison with differences in the provision of resources that are less movable, or quite immovable—land, climate, human skills, and even equipment. There is a wide range of industries—'light' industries in most senses of the term—that use so little fuel, power, or weight of materials per unit value of their product that their total costs are not much affected by differences from place to place in the prices of these things. These industries—textiles, clothing, light engineering (and a good many branches of engineering not usually classed as 'light'), rubber, some food trades, such as biscuits and cocoa can be set up in any inhabited part of the world with a facility which depends mainly upon the cost and skill of labour and the availability of capital and organizing-power. They are, in effect, 'footloose' industries, liable to be found wherever the basic requirements for modern forms of industrial organization exist, except for those areas which have an outstanding comparative advantage for some 'heavy' industry, for mining, or for agriculture.

Even these strong comparative advantages in the inevitably localized industries, indeed, do not entirely drive the 'footloose' industries out. One reason for this is that the 'footloose' character of some light industries is modified by an attraction to their markets, based not so much upon transport costs as upon the advantage of being in close touch with demand. The motor component and accessory trades could, so far as cost of production is concerned, equally well be almost anywhere in Great Britain, but in fact they are mainly in the Midlands, not far from the main assembly plants. The 'fashion goods' branches of the clothing industry tend to be situated in the big wealthy cities, like Paris, New York, and London, though any very large centre of population attracts them to some extent. The international distribution of all branches of economic activity is of course, great modified, mostly in the direction of bringing them nearer to their markets, by the existence of import taxes and other obstacles to trade.

That some 'footloose' industries are to be found almost anywhere (subject to difficulties that apply to any industry in undeveloped countries), does not, however, mean that they are all to be found in any one area. The mere fact that scale of production is important, and that, even in many of the 'light' industries, a single plant of economic size will supply the wants of a very large area, prevents this from being the case. Local specialization, as we have seen in the earlier part of this chapter, inevitably exists even when there is no strong economic reason why one place rather than another should have been selected originally for any one of many industries rather than another. This localization, moreover, is sometimes strongly reinforced by the tendency for similar plants to be established close together. There are sometimes economic reasons for this, but they have probably been given too much importance; it can often be shown that an established firm gets no tangible advantage from being near similar firms. Local specialization is often explicable only by reference to history; new firms are started by men from old firms who see no reason to move far away, and may also, in the early days of their enterprises, get benefits from being in the place where they have access to the gossip of the trade, and to a supply of labour used to working in it. Later on, when their firms have grown, they may be perfectly capable of training their own workpeople and as well able to exist in isolation as in the neighbourhood of others of their own kind; but unless there is some special reason for them to move, they stay where they are.

There is, therefore, a good deal of localization even among industries that are in principle 'footloose' though the reason for their being in the particular places where they are may sometimes be trivial. The industries which are not 'footloose' are, generally, much more strongly localized, and for more permanently effective reasons, which we have considered. Countries with poor supplies of capital and skill, or with inefficient political and legal systems may not be able to develop factory industry at all, even if other conditions (such as lack of agricultural resources, in proportion to the population) suggest that their comparative advantage lies ultimately in that direction. Bearing these general principles in mind, we may now turn to look at the broad pattern of specialization and trade in the world.

CHAPTER 10

The Pattern of International Trade

The Growth of Trade

THE pattern of international trade, as we know it today, and the main trends visible in it, are the result of developments which can best be understood by tracing them back for about a hundred years. In the middle of the nineteenth century, at the time of the Great Exhibition, the United Kingdom had attained a degree of pre-eminence in world trade from which she almost continuously fell away in the following hundred years, and which no other country equalled until the United States briefly held a similar position just after the second world war. Britain in 1851 was the source of between a quarter and a third of all the goods which were sent out across international frontiers—a fact which becomes the more impressive when we realize that, since trade is essentially an exchange, no one country can normally be responsible for more than half of the world export total.

Britain's exports in the 1850's were mainly the results of her industrial revolution; they were nearly all finished manufactures, two-thirds of them being either textiles or wrought iron products. Their physical volume, in the Exhibition year, were just about four times as great as it had been a generation before. In exchange for them, the United Kingdom got mainly raw materials, especially the materials for its textile industries—foodstuffs were as yet not of such great importance. In short, international trade was expanding at a great rate mainly because of the industrialization of the United Kingdom (and, to a smaller extent, of France, Belgium, and Germany), and consisted largely of an exchange of manufactured goods for raw materials and, to a smaller extent, for foodstuffs.

This development continued very fast in the following generation. The United Kingdom, as well as widening areas of Europe and the United States, developed their manufacturing industry, requiring ever-increasing amounts of raw materials from overseas. At the same time, the growth of British and other European populations outran the capacities of their home food supply, and foodstuffs became progressively more important in their countries' import-lists. As a complement to this, the building of railways in North and South

145

America, India, and other great continental areas of the world was opening them up so that they could profitably grow crops or mine minerals for export. Capital and (in the New World) colonists were flowing into them to help in this. Moreover, the steamship was cutting the cost of maritime transport, and there was a widespread movement towards the reduction of government restrictions and taxes on international trade. The result was a more than trebling of the volume of international trade within the generation, during which world production cannot have increased by much more than 50 per cent. or population by more than, perhaps, 20 per cent. The foundations of a new international division of labour were being laid.

To a large extent this process can be explained by saying that the cheapening of transport and the removal of barriers had made it possible, and profitable, for the areas with plenty of agricultural land or mineral deposits but little labour, to concentrate on the kinds of production that require that particular mixture of factors of production, while those areas with little land but much labour specialized on manufacturing industry, which does not require agricultural land, and does not depend, either, on the occurrence of any particular natural resources in its near neighbourhood, though a local supply of fuel is useful. This very simple explanation of the events in terms of comparative advantage is not, however, adequate. The densely populated countries of Asia, for instance, should, on this reckoning, have shared in the specialization on manufacturing so far, at least, as 'footloose' industries were concerned. Instead of this, not only did they show no industrialization in this period, but the handicrafts of India began to be undermined by importation of British cottons and other manufactures—a process which went further in the following generation. Comparative advantage can still be invoked, but as we have already seen, it is necessary to look beyond labour and fixed natural resources to the factors which are less permanent—the absence or presence of a supply of capital, of enterprise, and of technical knowledge and skill. That these, together with the political conditions which gave them a chance, existed in western Europe and not in India or China, in the middle of last century, was at least as important as the distribution of population and agricultural land in bringing about the particular pattern of specialization which we have noted.

By the 1870's, manufacturing was becoming more widespread. Whereas in 1850 the United Kingdom had been responsible for considerably more than half the world's manufactured exports, it provided only about 37 per cent. of them by the later 'seventies, and had, by then probably been surpassed in sheer volume of manufacturing production by the United States (which, however, was still only a minor exporter of these products). The volume of manufactured output in the world trebled between 1870 and 1900, and then doubled (despite the interruption of the first world war) by 1925. It trebled again by 1954. This is, of course, a much faster increase than agricultural production, or production as a whole, was showing; the proportion of world production which could be classed as manufactured was steadily increasing, and so was the number of countries which could be regarded as industrialized to a substantial degree.

We may say there has been a gradual spreading over more and more of the world of combinations of political conditions, skill, knowledge, enterprise and supply of capital which favoured industrialization. This has happened both to countries like Japan and (more recently) India, which are poor in natural resources in relation to the sizes of their populations, and to those like Canada and Australia, which are very rich in natural resources. Industrialization has happened, to some extent, nearly everywhere. Whether a country has become a net exporter of manufactured goods, however, has depended not only on its possession of the political and the 'mutable' economic conditions just mentioned which favour industrialization, but also on the relations of its natural resources to its population. Canada, Australia, and the Argentine in common with other countries of high income and well-developed economic institutions, have what is needed for industrialization, and have, indeed, undergone a good deal of industrial development, but because they have exceptional agricultural resources in relation to their populations they remain net exporters of agricultural produce and net importers of manufactures. Japan, on the other hand, lacking the facilities for producing food or raw materials for export on a large scale (with the exception of silk), became a net exporter of manufactures as long ago as 1913, and India, although slower in acquiring the capital and the skills needed for modern manufacturing, is on the brink of becoming one also.

Since the last quarter of the nineteenth century, it has, moreover, become increasingly misleading to think of trade as mainly an exchange of manufactured products for foodstuffs and raw materials. With the spread of industrialization, and also of highly specialized agriculture, there has also been a great increase in the exchange of some kinds of manufactured goods for others, and of some foodstuffs or raw materials for others. We shall return to this point later

It will be seen later too, that, when one industrial country exchanges certain kinds of manufactures or semi-finished goods with another, it does not normally do so much trade with it *in proportion to that other country's total output*, as it would if the other country were not industrialized. In the same way, a specialized primary-producing (i.e. agricultural or mining) country may trade with another one, but is likely to do less trade with it than it would do with an industrialized country having the same total value of output. The economist's way of expressing this is to say that an industrial country and a primary-producing one are generally more strongly complementary with each other than are two industrial or two primary-producing countries. The practical measure of complementarity is the amount of trade done in proportion to income—that is to say, in proportion to the amounts of goods and services which are produced, and therefore, in principle, available to be traded. We may take the proportion of the total output of the world which is internationally traded at any given time as a sort of general measure of the average degree of complementarity. Thus measured, complementarity was increasing, on the whole, not only from the eighteen-fifties to the 'seventies, but (though probably at a decreasing rate) until the 'nineties.

After a setback lasting about a decade, it rose again until the beginning of the first world war. Since then, there have been fluctuations, but world trade has never been so high in relation to world income as it was in 1913.

The Decline of International Complementarity

Granted that the first great spurt in the growth of complementarity came, as we have noted, from industrialization in a restricted part of the world and greatly improved communications with the rest of it, why did the process falter, then halt, then go into reverse? Five possible reasons suggest themselves. One is that the division of function between the first industrial countries and the others may have rested upon differences in their endowments with what we have called the 'mutable' factors—capital, knowledge, political security, and so on—rather than more permanent differences, and that these differences were subsequently removed or reduced. Alternatively, the ratio of population to permanent resources may have altered through migration or differences in rates of natural growth of population. Again, knowledge may have increased so as to reveal useful resources in places where they were either not known to exist or not known to be useful. Fourth, action may have been taken to obstruct or alter the flow of trade for reasons of policy. Or, finally, it may simply have happened that the more self-sufficient economies, with the lowest ratios of trade to income, increased their production faster than the others.

All five of these factors can be found at work—their net effect being, after the last decade of the nineteenth century, against the growth of complementarity; though they did not all work in that direction all the time. We have already noted that the spread of knowledge, of the availability of capital, and of the will to industrialize, had altered the trade pattern a good deal by the 'seventies, though up to then, and for some time longer, it probably worked to increase complementarity, not only by increasing the supply of manufactures for export from a limited number of countries, but by facilitating the development of transport, mining, commercial agriculture, and local processing of primary products for export in most other parts of the world. But where the country turns out to be good at producing manufactures for the home market, once it has got the necessary capital and skill, as happened in many European countries, in the United States, and later on, in Japan, there is likely to be a phase in which its imports grow less quickly than its income and may even fall in value. Even though it has to import machinery and raw, or semi-manufactured materials to make these goods, this will offset only a part of the value of the manufactured imports which its new products will enable it to dispense with—unless its industrialization proceeds at a rapidly increasing pace, keeping the imports of machinery ahead of the consequential import replacement. If it turns out to be so good at some kind of manufacture that it eventually enters the export market with it, however, the check to its foreign trade will be reversed, and it may expand again, even in relation to its expanding income. This stage seems to have been reached in the United States about the beginning of this century, at about the same time at which that country's exports classified as 'finished manufactures' became greater in total value than its imports which fell within the same class.

The increase in any primary producing country's population tends eventually to reduce its exports in relation to its output. Suppose that the whole population is engaged in growing food, part of which they export in exchange for clothing and other manufactures. As the population increases, a point will be reached at which poorer land has to be resorted to, or at which increasing labour per unit of land already in use brings decreasing returns. As average family income is reduced in this way, food consumption is likely to be cut by each family rather less than in proportion to this reduction; that is to say, a rather higher proportion of each family's product will be retained and a lower proportion, therefore, exported. If the economy manages to escape the effects of land-shortage by transferring some of its people into non-agricultural work, then agricultural production as a whole increases less than in proportion to total income, and, unless the new, non-agricultural work is itself in an exporting industry, so does foreign trade.

The effects of a development something like this have been important in many countries. Eastern Europe (including Russia) and India were both large grain exporters in the later part of last century; both ceased to become so because their populations increased and ate up the exportable grain surplus. Argentine meat exports have been reduced for a similar reason. So, since the beginning of this century, have food exports from the United States, apart from a temporary revival due to the first world war, and a rather longer-lived one due to the second. Up almost to the end of last century, the pressure of increasing population on the food resources of these countries was not heavy, because they had plenty of land to fall back upon. Moreover, because the populations of the industrial countries of Europe—and thus their demand for foodstuffs—were also growing fast, the inducement for the primary producing countries to export was expanding. From some point towards the end of last century, however, the filling-up of the overseas countries by immigration and natural increase of population began to take effect, and subsequently the rate of population growth in western Europe (and, for some time, in the United States as well) slowed down. These two developments tended on the one hand to make the supply of primary products from the overseas countries expand rather more slowly than their local income, and, on the other, to damp down the rate of increase in Europe's demand for primary products—the combined effect being to reduce the growth of trade in relation to the growth of income in the world as a whole. The contrast between the empty spaces of the new countries and the crowded populations of Europe is not quite so great as it was, and the case for a division of labour based upon this particular contrast is consequently not quite so strong.

Discovery of new natural resources has affected the pattern of international trade enormously in the last hundred years, but it seems probable that it has increased complementarity rather than diminished it. Perhaps the most momentous of these discoveries have been the great mineral finds. Broadly speaking, the early industrializations were built upon home sources of minerals, materials and fuels—especially coal. The industrialized countries knew their own mineral resources, in general, before they knew those of other countries, and they exploited them first. Prospecting and discovery have therefore tended to be increasingly in the less industrialized, and less known parts of the world—and have resulted in very much increased trade between them and the more developed areas. The huge trade in middle eastern and Venezuelan oil is the most important case in point. It probably outweighs all the reductions in trade through smaller mineral discoveries which have enabled home products to be substituted for imports. On the other side of the account, however, we have to put the technological discoveries which have enabled countries to dispense with imports—the discovery of how to substitute the nitrogen of the air for Chilean nitrates, or how to substitute derivatives of widely-occurring materials like wood and coal for imported commodities like cotton, silk, or indigo, or how to use water-power instead of imported coal. Nevertheless, it would probably be reasonable to guess that the geological and technological discoveries of the last hundred years, taken together, have tended to increase, rather than to decrease, not only the volume of international trade, but the degree of international complementarity in the world economy.

Trade Barriers
The fourth factor which we have mentioned—interference with trade for reasons of policy—certainly worked in the other direction. Import tariffs—taxes on imports—have been important throughout most of history. The middle part of last century, however, was a time in which they were very widely reduced, or, in some important countries, largely abandoned. The United Kingdom led this movement towards free trade. At that time her manufacturers had relatively little to fear from foreign competition in the home market; Britain really was, as we have noted, in a large degree the 'workshop of the world', and they favoured a policy which seemed likely to help in opening foreign markets to their products. As for agricultural products, there was a bitter struggle between those who favoured the retention of import duties on them—the landlords and farmers—and the mainly urban and industrial interests who wanted their abolition, and industrialization had already gone far enough in the eighteen-forties for the abolitionists to win. The great expansion of trade in the third quarter of the century was materially helped by the British free trade movement and its repercussions abroad.

But this did not last. As people in other countries, sometimes with the active encouragement of the state, sought to set up factory industries on the lines pioneered mainly in the United Kingdom, they came more and more to seek shelter from the competition of Britain's and later of each other's exports. Moreover, from the eighteen-seventies onwards, when railways had opened up the new grain-growing lands of America and Russia, European agriculture faced competition of a most drastic kind. In the United Kingdom, agricultural interests were no longer strong enough to protest effectively, and few people were alarmed at the strategic implications of the country's becoming very heavily dependent on imports for its food supply. On the continent, however, the position was vastly different. The farming communities there were still politically very important and, for countries that had not naval command of their sea-routes, dependance upon overseas trade for essential food supplies entailed a heavy political risk. In most European countries, therefore, a move towards higher taxation of agricultural imports began. These general tendencies towards protection of particular industrial and agricultural interests against foreign competition have operated sporadically ever since in most countries.

At certain times, however, they have been assisted by special forces. Both of the world wars in the present century have interrupted the normal flow of international trade and have therefore given both industry and agriculture in many countries very special temporary protection against foreign competition—offset, to some extent, by the difficulty which the very same stoppage of trade put in the way of many industries expanding their equipment to meet the opportunities. To some extent, the development in the direction of greater self-sufficiency which the circumstances of war had fostered (despite the difficulties just mentioned) proved to be permanent. Industries, or branches of agriculture, once established, in many cases persisted when peace returned, either with or without the help of tariffs—though sometimes, as with British agriculture after the first world war, the removal of the wartime stimulus meant the reversal of wartime growth.

The great depression of the nineteen-thirties brought an even bigger move away from free trade. The reason in that period was not so much a desire to protect or foster particular branches of each country's economic activity, though that was present, too. In some cases it was a need to save currency reserves, as depression elsewhere reduced the amount of money that could be earned by exporting. In others it was a desire to 'export unemployment' by obliging the population to buy home-produced goods instead of imports. It was at this time that the United Kingdom departed from her historic free trade policy of the preceding eighty years.

The second world war and its aftermath brought another great crop of trade restrictions quite apart from the inevitable wartime interruption of trade which we have just mentioned. The principal reason for these was that nearly every country in the world outside

North America found itself with urgent need of imports and plenty of its own money to spend on them, but with a very much smaller capacity to provide goods to sell in exchange. As in the depression of the 'thirties, therefore, barriers (mainly quotas and licensing systems rather than taxes) were raised to keep imports within the limits set by current earnings of foreign currency, reserves which could be drawn upon, and help which could be got in the form of gifts or loans.

At first these restrictions on imports were largely indiscriminate, but they were gradually modified by agreements between pairs of countries, or by 'liberalization'—the removal of restrictions other than import duties—between countries outside North America, and especially inside Europe. The production difficulties and the pressures of internal demand which had restricted exports, particularly from European countries, gradually abated; consequently, from 1950, the world entered upon a period in which trade grew faster than income though it still remained a good deal smaller in relation to total production than it had been before the war.

It is extremely difficult to compare the general level of barriers to international trade now with what it was, say, in 1925 or 1913; taking the world as a whole it may still be higher than at either of those dates, but even if it were (or were soon to become) no higher, it would still remain true that the second world war and its aftermath, like the first, would be found to have given the structure of production a permanent push in the direction of less international complementarity.

Over the last generation, however, the final factor which we have mentioned—the greater growth of the more self-sufficient economies as compared with these more dependent upon trade—has probably been one of the main forces reducing the ratio of trade to income in the world as a whole. The United States and the Soviet Union are among the most self-sufficient economies, with only a few per cent. of their outputs entering international trade. Since 1929, American national income has more than doubled and Russian probably more than trebled, whereas world income as a whole probably rose by only about three-quarters. It has been, increasingly, an age of big economies, and since the big economies are naturally less dependent upon the outside world than small ones, this must tend to diminish the ratio of trade to production.

The Changing Composition of Trade

The composition of world trade has changed over the years partly because of the changing nature of the goods which are produced, partly because of changes in the degree of complementarity between countries—that is to say, changes in the extent to which they produce goods other than those which they themselves want. Let us try to look at these two influences separately.

We have already seen that, during the last century or more, production of manufactured goods has grown much more rapidly than agricultural production, and that this has been reflected in a greater growth of trade in manufactures than of trade in agricultural products (or primary products generally). The exchange of manufactured for primary products, which was probably at one time most of world trade, is now less than half of it, while a quarter of world trade (a growing proportion) consists of the exchange of one kind of manufactures for another. Over a shorter period—the last generation —we can follow the process in greater detail.

The commodity classes which have claimed expanding proportions of world trade over that period are machinery, scientific instruments, metals and ores, transport equipment, chemicals, and petroleum. In the middle nineteen-twenties they constituted about a quarter of the value of world trade; now they constitute more than half of it. It seems certain that these are all classes of goods production of which has grown faster than world production as a whole; in the United States for instance, while total production (real income produced) rather more than doubled over the period in question, output of chemicals as a whole quadrupled and that of both machinery and transport equipment more than trebled, as indeed, did *world* production of petroleum. At the other end of the scale stand rubber manufactures (mostly tyres), clothing, textiles, cereals, and beverages, which (with a few smaller classes) constituted half international trade in the middle 'twenties, but are only a quarter of it now. Some, though not all of these, are goods the production of which failed to keep pace with world production as a whole. We know, for instance, that world production of cotton and rayon textiles (which together are about four-fifths of all textiles) rose by only something like a third over this period, whereas world production of goods of all kinds taken together must have risen by about 75 per cent. Cereal production rose even less—probably only by about a quarter. On the other hand, production of rubber manufactures certainly rose more than world output as a whole; the relative decline of this category in world trade must have been wholly due to the setting up of factories in countries which had previously imported their tyres. It is known too, that the decline (which is absolute as well as relative to world trade) in exports of textiles, while partly explained by the relatively slow growth of world demand for these products, is not wholly explained by it. Trade in cotton and rayon textiles fell from 27 per cent. of world production of them in 1926-8 to only 14 per cent. in 1951. The growth of textile industries in China, India, and other former importing countries is responsible for this.

Between the kinds of good which have done best and those which have done worst in world trade, there stand some intermediate classes which have about kept pace with the total, claiming together something over a sixth throughout the last thirty years. They include wood, paper, and most of the main kinds of foodstuff except cereals. Production of paper and newsprint has probably expanded about as much as production in general; production of wood and most of the foodstuffs in question have expanded less. Though these commodities have done about as well in world trade as all commodities taken together, it should be remembered that the trade as a whole has not managed to keep up with production; a great depression and a great war (especially the former) have each given development a twist in the direction of self-sufficiency.

The present position is that food, drink, and tobacco amount to about 17 per cent. of total world trade (by value), against something like 23 per cent. in the nineteen-twenties; raw materials (including animal and vegetable oils and fats) are about 14 per cent. as compared with nearly 20 per cent. thirty years ago. Mineral fuels have gone up from 5 to $7\frac{1}{2}$ per cent.—the advance of oil having been greater than the retreat of coal. Chemicals have gone up from 3 to 5 per cent. Machinery and transport equipment have gone up from 9 per cent. to over 20. Other manufactures have come down from 32 to 26 per cent. of the world total, chiefly because of the great fall of textiles and clothing from 15 to under 7 per cent. of it. All manufactures together, including chemicals, have, however, risen from 44 to 52 per cent. of the total, while foodstuffs, raw materials, and fuels have fallen from 48 to 38 per cent. of it.

Industrialization and the basis of the Trade Pattern
This shift towards manufactures reflects the increased industrialization of the world, which carries with it increased real income and a reduction in the proportion of income spent on food. It is also due, in some measure, to the fact that many of the goods which are of increased importance in international trade and production generally (motor cars, for instance) are of higher value in relation to the raw materials which go into them than is the case with textiles, which were formally of greater importance relatively to other goods than they are now. In other words, more is added by manufacture to

the raw materials in the newer industries than in the older ones, so that the demand for raw materials tends to increase less than the demand for finished goods. Increased (and more widespread) industrialization involves an increase in the extent to which trade consists of an exchange of one kind of manufacture for another between countries both of which are in some degree industrialized.

If we exclude the Soviet bloc (for which the corresponding information is not available), it appears that international trade in 1954 was made up as follows:

	% of world trade
Manufactures from one industrial country to another ...	22
Primary products from one industrial country to another ...	15
Manufactures from industrial to non-industrial countries	19
Primary products from non-industrial to industrial countries	24
All goods from one non-industrial country to another ...	10

In this classification (by the Contracting Parties to the General Agreement on Tariffs and Trade), the industrial countries are taken to be those of western Europe, together with Japan, the United States and (perhaps rather surprisingly in this context) Canada. If it is accepted, it emerges that the industrial countries sell more manufactures to each other than to non-industrial countries and, indeed, get more than three-fifths as much primary products from each other as they get from the primary producing countries. There is, however, nothing anomalous about this; one must remember that the industrial countries, as defined here, are much bigger producers, in aggregate, than the rest—on a rough calculation, three or four times as big. It can be seen from the table that the total trade they do between themselves (the sum of the first two items) is also between three and four times as great as the trade from one to another of the non-industrial countries. On this evidence, the industrial countries are about as complementary with each other as the non-industrial countries are. But since the trade that they do with the non-industrial countries (the third and fourth items in the table, plus some minor quantities of primary products exported from industrial to non-industrial countries, and manufactures sent in the opposite direction) is considerably greater than their trade with each other, in spite of the amount which the primary producers have to offer being so much less, it is clear that the degree of complementarity between industrial and non-industrial countries is greater than that between those within either of these two broad classes—which is as one would expect.

For all kinds of goods, lumped together, this kind of analysis can usefully be taken further, by dividing the world into a greater number of convenient areas—North America, the European sterling area (the British Isles and Iceland), continental western Europe, the overseas sterling area (Burma, Iraq, and the British Commonwealth, excluding Canada and the United Kingdom), Latin America, the Soviet bloc, Japan, and the rest of the world. Over a quarter of international trade takes place within, rather than between these areas. The quantity obviously depends on how they happen to be internally divided up—continental western Europe, for instance, which (on this definition) consists of thirteen countries, has a huge internal trade which amounts to about a seventh of the world total; that the internal trade of North America is only half as big as this is partly due to the fact that only two countries are involved, Japan, being classified as an area by herself in this particular division of the world, has obviously no internal international trade at all. For all the areas here distinguished, however, except the Soviet bloc, external trade is greater than that within the area, and it is this interregional trade which is most interesting.

The two big components of interregional trade which stand out on first inspection are that between the European and non-European parts of the sterling area, and that between North and Latin America, each being just under a tenth of all international trade. The trade between North American and the whole of western Europe is only slightly less (two-thirds of it with the Continent, one-third with the British Isles). Continental western Europe's trades with the overseas sterling area and Latin America are each about 4 per cent. of the international trade total; the overseas sterling area's trade with North America is rather under 3 per cent. of it. No other stream of trade which can be given a simple geographical description is big compared with these.

When we come to examine these main streams of trade in relation to the amounts of goods which are produced, and therefore in principle available to be traded, we learn a good deal about both the different degrees of self-sufficiency and the different degrees of complementarity of the various regions of the world. North America, the European sterling area, and continental western Europe do not differ much in the amounts of goods they import from outside themselves, and North America exceeds the other two by only about 40 per cent. in the amount it exports, though its income is two or three times that of western continental Europe, and perhaps six or seven times that of the European sterling area. Density of population has probably more to do with this great difference in self-sufficiencies than anything else. All three areas have to import tropical products, but North America has to import only a few raw materials and fuels whereas continental Europe has to import many more and the British Isles more still, while continental Europe relies on impor- tation for some of its non-tropical foodstuffs, and the British Isles for most of them.

We have already seen that the industrial areas of the world import higher proportions of the products of primary producing areas than of other industrial regions, and this is confirmed by a more detailed analysis. North America, for instance, imports nearly three times as much from Latin America and the overseas sterling area together as it does from the whole of western Europe and Japan, despite the fact that the industrial areas just mentioned produce 60 per cent. more than the two great primary producing regions. In the same way the British Isles import 25 per cent. more from these two primary producing regions than from North America, western conti- nental Europe and Japan, which together produce about four times as much. Broadly speaking, an industrial region seems to import between two-and-a-half and five times as much from primary producing areas generally as from other industrial areas generally, in proportion to what they produce. The preference of Latin America and the overseas sterling area for goods from the industrial areas rather than goods from each other is, in relation to relative outputs, even more pronounced.

But it is very far from being true that this high degree of com- plementarity, as evidenced by the trade pattern, is to be found between any industrial area and every single primary producing region—still less between it and all primary producing areas equally. The British Isles import a higher proportion of the output of western continental Europe than of that of Latin America, while North America imports only a slightly higher proportion of the product of the overseas sterling area than of the product of the British Isles. The primary product buying of the British Isles, in fact, is very heavily concentrated upon the sterling area, and so is that of North America (especially the United States) upon Latin America. Continental Europe distributes its buying more evenly between the two—but with some bias towards the overseas sterling area. It takes, however, a smaller proportion of the outputs of either of these primary producing areas than it does of that of the British Isles.

These differences are matters partly of history and politics, partly of geography. The concentration of British buying of primary com- modities on the sterling area results partly from long trade connection, personal contacts, and the development of the overseas sterling area in a deliberate relation to the United Kingdom market, partly on Imperial Preference, and partly on currency regulations in the years since the war, when the United Kingdom (like many other areas) was not earning enough dollars to buy as much as it would otherwise have bought in the Americas. The North American concentration on Latin America is rather less pronounced—the factors of tariff preference and currency difficulty are not present in this case; but since the first world war much development there has been financed from the United States, and related to the United States market. It is also natural that, if Europeans for whatever reasons buy sterling area goods, Americans, without having any preference for those from outside the sterling area, will find their buying concentrated on them.

The fairly strong North American connection with the United Kingdom is largely due to Canada's having developed, like the rest of the Commonwealth in quite close connection with the British market, and also, again, to Imperial Preference. On the other hand, the close trading relations, in both directions, between the British Isles and the Continent are largely a matter of proximity. They are to a considerable extent, though not entirely, bound up with the exchange of semi-finished or finished manufactures of one kind for those of others; the Scandinavian timber, the Danish, Dutch, and French farm produce and the French wine also come into the picture. The North Sea and the Channel are not very formidable barriers to trade.

The Part of Multilateral Exchange

This brief description of the pattern of trade has dealt with pairs of areas without raising the question whether trade between the members of each pair is the same in both directions. In fact, it is not; provided that the world is divided into more than two regions for the purpose of the analysis, there is no reason why trade between one region and another should exactly balance, and usually good reasons why it should not. A country will not necessarily sell its specialities to the same countries which are best able to supply it with the things in which it is deficient. There is, indeed, some tendency for big and relatively unspecialized countries to have their imports more concentrated both in kind and geographically than their exports, and for small and specialized countries to be in the opposite position. The United States, for instance, has such a wide range of both manufactured and primary exports that it is not surprising to find them fairly evenly spread over the world; its imports, on the other hand, are rather highly concentrated under such headings as tropical products and certain minerals, which come predominantly from particular parts of the world, This means that, so long as United States imports and exports as a whole balance, there is bound to be an excess of imports over exports with some areas (e.g. tropical countries) and an excess of exports over imports in trade with others. This is, indeed, the traditional pattern of United States trade—a large surplus of exports to Canada, Europe and the temperate Latin American countries over imports from them, and an excess of imports from most tropical and certain mineral-producing countries over exports to them. In recent years this pattern has been modified by the tendency of the United States to have its exports as a whole greatly in excess of its imports. If we take exports and imports of services, as well as of goods, into account, moreover, the pattern, for recent years, is modified by the large military expenditures of the United States in Europe—which have given both the United Kingdom and western continental Europe more dollars from United States sources than they have spent on United States goods and services.

Canada provides an even more striking example. Since a good deal of her exports are agricultural products of the kinds that the United Kingdom, but not (to the same extent) the United States requires to import, and since, for her manufactured imports, she has the readiest access to the United States market, she naturally tends to have a surplus of her transactions with the United Kingdom and a deficit on those with the United States. The United Kingdom, indeed, spends in Canada (and to a smaller extent in certain Central and South American countries), a good deal more than the surplus of dollars which in recent years she has received in her direct dealings with the United States. With the 'Dollar Area' as a whole, therefore, she has a debit balance, which is made up, so far as she is concerned, by her large credit balance with the rest of the sterling area, and, so far as the sterling area as a whole is concerned, by sales of Malayan tin and rubber, West African cocoa, and South African gold to the dollar countries.

In the same way, Germany before the war and western Germany now tend to have a credit balance with other continental European countries, chiefly because German products are largely manufactures of the kinds that are bought by other industrial countries; with the overseas sterling area and some other countries from which they import much of the raw materials and foodstuffs, they have normally had debit balances.

The international pattern of trade and payments is thus a very complicated one, and even if each country's payments to the rest of the world as a whole for currently-received goods and services exactly balanced its current receipts from the rest of the world—that is to say, if no country were borrowing from or lending to any other—it would still not follow, by any means, that each country's payments with any other country, singly, would be in balance. To use the terms which are generally employed, a country's settlement for the goods and services it buys from another country may well be multi-lateral (involving other countries) rather than bilateral (involving only the two of them). This, of course, is the normal state of affairs between families or firms within an economy. Most families derive their income by selling services to one or two employers, from whom they may well buy nothing. They spend it, immediately with quite a large number of retail firms and providers of services, and, ultimately, with a vastly greater number of producers throughout the world. Most of the settlements between families or firms are therefore multilateral—it is for that reason that money, a generally acceptable means of payment, is necessary, and barter unworkable.

When we come to deal with large aggregates, such as national economies, it becomes more likely that the transactions between any pair of them will come near to balance, since economies are less specialized in their provision of goods and services than families or firms—both members of the pair are likely to be able to produce for export so many different kinds of thing that the trade between them will probably not be all, or nearly all, in one direction. With the fifteen countries which were members of the European Payments Union, it was found that the total bilateral balances—the total of the amounts by which one country bought more from another than it sold to it—ran as high as £1,100 million a year, which was something like a fifth of the total trade between the countries concerned. If we take five major areas of the world—North America, South America, the British Isles, west continental Europe (with its overseas dependencies) and the overseas sterling area—we find that the sum of the bilateral balances between them is still something over £1,000 million, which is, however, only about a fifteenth of the total value of goods and services moving between them in a year. These bilateral balances, both between the countries of Europe and between the big major trading regions of the world, included a good deal of borrowing by particular countries (or areas) from all the rest put together. They were partly due to the fact that trade was out of balance, and only partly therefore, also, to the genuinely multilateral pattern of settlements.

In view of this, it may seem that the extent to which the pattern

L

of payments in international trade is multilateral is surprisingly small. There are, in fact, a number of pressures making for bilateral balance. In the first place, trade and indeed the development of sources of supply on which trade depends, often arise because knowledge of the possibilities, personal connections, and a supply of credit happen to exist. If these factors are brought into existence through the growth of trade from A to B, they are likely to promote also the growth of trade from B to A. Secondly, some kinds of transport—railways and liner shipping, for instance—tend to promote two-way trade; if they are called upon to carry a heavy traffic in one direction, there will obviously be a good (and probably a very cheap) service for goods going the other way.

These two, so to speak, 'natural' causes have a good deal to do with the two-way nature of trade between the British Isles and the rest of the sterling area, or between the United States and Latin America. But bilateralism has been greatly assisted by other things, most of which have been mentioned already in a slightly different connection—tariff preference (such as Imperial Preference), the breakdown or dislocation of the international payments system in the great depression of the 'thirties and the second world war, and, finally, the development of the centrally planned economies largely in isolation from the rest of the world. To the extent that these or other factors prevent the pattern of trade from being multi-lateral, they restrict opportunities for exchanges which could be generally beneficial; but it is not possible to say how far the pattern of settlements 'ought' to be multilateral, or would be multilateral in the absence of constraints. There is no special virtue in the size of multilateral settlements as such—or, indeed, in the size of international trade as such. The course of economic development, supposing it to be such as to make the best of changes in knowledge and of human and physical circumstances, might increase the degree in which the pattern of payments is multilateral, or decrease it, just as it might either increase or decrease international trade as a whole in relation to world income.

Indeed, the most general conclusion to be drawn from the facts surveyed in this chapter is that the pattern of international trade depends upon the distribution about the world, not only of the relatively immobile factors of production land and labour, but, at least as much, of what we have called the 'mutable' factors, which play a key part in economic development. It is therefore subject to continuous and radical change, in which purely artificial barriers also exercise a large (sometimes a commanding) function. For communities which depend heavily upon it, adaptability and innovation are essential to well-being, if not to survival. The hazards against which this adaptability is their main defence are, indeed, common to all participants in any but the most primitive economy; we must now look more closely at these and other hazards of economic life.

CHAPTER 11

The Hazards of Economic Life

Natural Causes

WE have now looked at the main factors which seem to determine the growth and present shapes of economies, and the nature of their trading relations with each other. From what we have seen it is not difficult to deduce some of the eventualities which may make for alteration in an economy's fortunes. In the first place, obviously enough, its fortunes may change because the amount of its production changes. So far as the development of its power to produce is concerned, what has been said here about growth must suffice; in the shorter run also, however, the amount it is able to produce will often vary from year to year mainly from natural causes such as weather. For an agricultural economy this is a very considerable hazard. The average change between one year and the next in the amount of wheat obtained per acre harvested in the United Kingdom, for instance, is nearly 10 per cent.—about as often a decrease as an increase—and is sometimes as high as 20 or 30 per cent. For many crops and many countries the year-to-year variation is much greater than this.

Where the economy in question sells some of its agricultural products outside, there is a further hazard, in that total supplies reaching the market in which it sells are, like its particular contribution, liable to variation, which will normally cause a variation in the price it receives per unit of the physical quantity it sells. The world wheat harvest for instance, changes from one year to the next by an average amount of 5 or 6 per cent., upwards or downwards, with occasional changes of more than 15 per cent. A big total harvest will lower the price; a small total harvest will raise it. If the harvest in the country or region we are considering varies in much the same way as the total supplies reaching the market in which it sells, then the fluctuations in the physical amount it has to sell will tend to be in the opposite direction from those in the price it realizes per unit, and its total earnings will thus be to some extent stabilized. If, as often happens, however, there is not much relation between, say a particular country's wheat harvest and the world harvest, then there will be years when a local glut combined with a world shortage

164

produce very large earnings, and others when a local shortage combined with a world surplus produce very low ones. For all the producers of an agricultural commodity considered together, it is usually true that a decrease in output is more than offset in its effect on total earnings by the increase in price per unit to which it gives rise—a fact which helps to explain the popularity at various times of the restriction schemes which were referred to in Chapter 5. Shortages are usually good for the suppliers; they are, by the same token, bad for economies which are net importers of the commodity in question. Variability in crop-yield introduces fluctuation into the fortunes, not only of the economies which export part of their crops, but of others as well.

So much for variation in supply—mostly from natural causes—as a source of year-to-year variation in incomes. Changes in demand are equally important. Some of these changes relate to only one commodity or one economy's output of it—and some are general. Let us look at them in that order.

Technology, Taste, and Competition

Changes in the kinds of goods which people want to buy are going on all the time; some are consequences of what can without doubt be called economic or technical progress, others of what can, more guardedly, only be called changes in fashion. Technical progress reduced the demand for horses, harness, candles, vegetable dyestuffs, cinema orchestras, and natural silk, though in the expanding world economy instances like these of an absolute fall in the demand for a class of good are not so numerous or so catastrophic as one might suppose. Changes in the method of producing a good have sometimes been more spectacular in that they have drastically reduced the demand for a particular kind of labour. The British handloom weavers—more than half a million of them—who were mostly displaced by the power loom in the second quarter of last century, provide one of the most distressing examples; a smaller one was the replacement of hand combers of wool by combing machines in the 1850's.

The fear of this kind of change and its consequent 'technological' unemployment hangs heavily over the later nineteen-fifties because of widespread discussion and anticipation of 'automation'. It seems that the changes which are included under that rather comprehensive head may very well diminish the total demand (at any rate in the countries already highly advanced industrially) for men and women in certain kinds of job, both manual and clerical, even though a good many of the more spectacular economies in labour are likely to be in industries like motors, radio, and household equipment which can be expected to experience relatively rapid increases in demand for their products, and have, indeed, hitherto been increasing their demand for manpower faster than others. If this is so, there will have to be adjustments and shifts, which some of the people involved will not like, and which may involve some unemployment for them. But there is no reason to expect that these hazards will be heavy in comparison with similar ones in the past. Advanced economies are always changing and the particular changes which are in question here, like others of their kind, cannot be introduced overnight; their speed depends on the rate at which old equipment is replaced by new, and at which more automatic techniques are worked out which save in cost as compared with less automatic ones. If automation could be expected to be introduced only in manufacturing industry, some idea of the change it might bring about in the British economy, for instance, might be gained by comparing the occupational structure of the United Kingdom with that of the United States—the main difference between the two, as we have seen, arising from the superior productivity of American labour in manufacturing. A rise in the productivity of British labour in manufacturing would, presumably, make the British occupational structure more like the American is now, with probably a somewhat (but not much) smaller proportion of the occupied population in manufacturing (and a rather higher proportion of those in the capital goods industries), and a higher proportion of the population in the various 'service' occupations. But this is too simple; automation is likely to exert some of its biggest labour-saving effects on office work, and will therefore probably tend to reduce the proportion of the occupied population which will be needed in finance and commerce, as well as in manufacturing.

Changes in consumers' tastes are a second source of hazard for producers; they are, however, not always easy to disentangle from changes in methods of production. In the 1870's for instance, demand shifted away from rather stiff and shiny (frequently black) kinds of women's dress materials towards softer cloths and more varied colours. How far was this a spontaneous change in taste, and how far was it stimulated by new techniques of weaving and cloth-finishing, and by the availability of the new synthetic dyestuffs? Whatever the answer might be, it is clear that a change in preferences plays a considerable part in such movements. Sometimes, indeed, as with the movement to much lighter clothing (especially for women) which took place in the nineteen-twenties, the brief vogue of ostrich-feathers which stimulated a short-lived South African industry at the beginning of this century, or the outmoding of mahogany furniture, which had severe effects on some of the Caribbean countries, the shift in demand is the main partner in the total change.

Fashion, in the sense of convention in matters connected with the appearance (as distinct from the rest of the function) of consumers' goods is, indeed, of very great economic importance—not only in the clothing and furniture industries. It is said that motor cars are chosen as much for their 'styling' as for their capacity and performance. In all trades affected by fashion, change in the design of the product is the essence of its appeal; buyers who aspire to be leaders of fashion aim always to have goods of slightly different design from those possessed by most people, and most others regard themselves as losing prestige if they lag too far behind. Since the tendency is for fashion to favour only one basic style at a time (or, at the most, to divide its favours among a few basic styles), and since changes in fashion are usually fairly rapid in relation to the time which it takes to design and produce goods, it is very important for producers in the markets in question to be clever, or lucky, in anticipating tastes.

Both the hazards from technological change, and the hazards from general change in taste have perhaps been less spectacular than those which arise simply in the course of world economic development from geographical spread of social and economic conditions which favour particular kinds of production. The eclipse of the Brazilian rubber industry by the plantation industry in Malaya and the Netherlands Indies in the first generation of this century is one example. Another—perhaps the most striking there has been—is the eclipse of the Lancashire cotton industry, in its overseas markets, by rivals, particularly Indian and Japanese. In 1912, the industry exported nearly seven-eighths of the cloth produced. By 1955, its cloth exports had declined to less than a tenth of their former quantity. Consequently, although sales in the home market had risen by two-thirds since 1912, total production had fallen to less than a third of what it was then, even if the expanding production of cloth made wholly or partly from artificial fibres is included. Total employment in the cotton spinning, doubling and weaving industries fell by not much short of two-thirds in the same period (it should be noted that yarn production declined rather less than that of cloth). For a great industry initially employing over 600,000 people, this is a catastrophic story. It exemplifies on the grand, or international scale, what is constantly happening in the world economy and in its component national and regional economies as one productive unit, or group of units, for some reason supplants another producing similar goods. On the international scale, however, the hazard is especially great, because a national industry which builds up a large export trade, as the British cotton textile industry did, is capable of being ruined not only by superior efficiency elsewhere, but also by governmental restrictions upon imports.

The Mechanism of Depression

The three types of hazard at which we have briefly looked—technological changes in production, changes in consumers' tastes, and successful competition (with or without the help of government protection) from similar producers elsewhere—have two important features in common; they are to a large extent inevitable in the ordinary course of economic development and progress, and they can in some degree be dodged by the individual producer in so far as he is able to be quick in adopting new techniques, changing the design of his product in conformity with changes in the market, and moving entirely, if need be, from one industry into another. The fact that these adjustments cannot in practice be made quickly by all concerned—some of them, indeed are inevitably painfully slow—does not alter the importance of this as a statement of principle. It is useful to distinguish these hazards from those of another kind, which could not be avoided by individual adaptability, namely the hazards which result not from the transfer of demand from products of one kind (or one provenance) to those of another, but from a reduction in aggregate demand for all products taken together. The effects of *shifts* in demand are, as we have just noted, in principle escapable by anyone who manages to be sufficiently adaptable, but the shifts themselves are inevitable if there is to be progress; on the other hand, recessions of total demand do not seem to be in principle inevitable (though they may, of course, be usual features of economies organized in certain particular ways), but where they exist their effects cannot be avoided by the exercise of adaptability—people cannot dodge from the occupations or places where demand is falling to those where it is increasing, because the latter either do not exist at all, or are less numerous than the former. We must now look at the sources of these troublesome reductions in total demand.

In order to do this, it will be necessary to recall what was said about the mechanism of exchange in Chapter 3. It was explained there that a constant rate of production and sale of goods and services can be maintained in an economy, at constant prices, provided that there is no net leakage of money out of or into active circulation.[1]

If there is a leakage out of circulation, it will be recalled, the result must be that there is an equivalent piling-up of unsold goods in the shops, or a reduction in the prices they will fetch, or both. Either, or both, of these results is likely to lead to a reduction in orders to producers, or a diminution of their incentives to produce—at all events, to a reduction in output. Similarly, if there is a net flow of money into active circulation, the result will be either an increase in sales which will deplete stocks in the shops, or a rise in the price which the goods on sale will fetch, or both. This will lead to increased orders to producers, or stronger incentives to produce, and thus (unless there are bottlenecks in the supply of factors of production which prevent it), to increased output. If therefore, we want to investigate the conditions under which there may be a net reduction in the total demand for an economy's products, we must look at the possible ways in which money can leak out of its active circulation.

We saw that there are two possible destinations of such a leakage; money may go from the active circulation either into inactive stocks within the economy (i.e. into what we agreed to call its capital market) or into the outside world—into the hands of residents outside the economy in question. Leakage from the active circulation into the hands of non-residents can happen only through a discrepancy between purchases of goods and services from abroad and exports of goods and services from the economy—a net excess of imports constitutes a leakage, a net excess of exports brings money into the active circulation. Internal leakage—leakage from active circulation into the capital market—comes about when the total expenditure of the community on new home-produced goods and services falls short of the total incomes which are being earned in the production of such goods and services, other than those which are for export.

If, therefore, we find ourselves faced with a net reduction in demand for the economy's goods and services, with its consequences of a reduction in orders for production, or a reduction in prices, or both, the first step in seeking its cause is to ask whether exports have fallen, whether imports have been substituted by purchasers within the country for home-produced goods, or whether one of the sections

---

[1] We should perhaps note here the additional condition that a constant rate of production will be maintained only if the levels of prices, and therefore of profits, begin by being such as to induce the various producing units to keep their rates of output unchanged—or, if they change them to do so by increasing output of one good and lowering that of another in ways which keep the *total* value of production at the existing prices unchanged.

of home demand for home-produced goods and services has fallen off, leading to a net accumulation of savings. The sections of this home demand which it is useful to distinguish will vary with the nature of the economy in question, and the completeness of the information we have about it, but it is often convenient to deal separately with private consumption (sometimes further distinguishing between non-durable goods, durable goods and services), public purchases of goods and services, and private investment expenditure —distinguishing if possible between purchases of new fixed capital and net additions to stocks of materials or goods held by producing or distributing enterprises.

In looking at these components of total demand, it will be convenient to start with private consumption, because a plausible assumption can be made about it which greatly simplifies the discussion of questions connected with demand and the level of economic activity. This assumption is that the amount of money which the people in an economy spend on consumers' goods and services is simply and closely related to their total income—or, at least, to their total income available after paying income tax and similar direct taxes. Suppose, for instance, that in a certain economy people always spend four-fifths of their income and save one-fifth. and let us suppose, also, for simplicity, that in this economy both public expenditure and external trade are negligible, so that the national income consists only of private consumption and investment. Now, we know that the level of income will be steady only if the total expenditure in the economy in any period is equal to the incomes which the spenders have received immediately beforehand. This can be the case in the simplified economy we are discussing only if what is spent on investment goods in any period equals what is saved (i.e. not spent on consumers' goods) out of the income received immediately beforehand—spending on consumers' goods and investment goods together must equal the income just received if income is to be kept at the same level in the next period also.

We can say, therefore, that if income is to remain steady, investment expenditure must be equal to one-fifth of income—or to put it the other way about, that income must always be equal to five times investment expenditure. If it is greater than this, then saving (which we have assumed really to be one-fifth of income) will exceed it, and there will be a leakage of purchasing-power out of active circulation, carrying with it a reduction in production or prices or both. If income is less than five times investment expenditure, then the latter will be greater than saving, and the active circulation will be increased with the help of money drawn from the money-market stock. On the assumption we have made—that exactly one-fifth of income is always saved, or four-fifths spent on consumption—every change in investment expenditure will be followed by a change five times as great in the income level. Having assumed that the part of income spent on consumption is rigidly governed by the level of income just received, we must not be surprised to find that the other component of expenditure—investment—appears now to be the one which, by its independent variations, is capable of ruling what the level of income is to be.

Is the assumption realistic—is the proportion of an economy's income which is spent on consumers' goods really constant? If we take averages for whole decades, we find that for some economies there is a fairly high degree of constancy over considerable periods. In the United States, for instance, the proportion of total national income *saved* was not lower than 10·4 per cent. or higher than 12 per cent. in any decade from the 1880's to the 1920's—but it fell catastrophically to 3 or 4 per cent. in the depressed decade of the 'thirties.

But constancy in the division of income between consumption and investment over long periods taking one year with another, is not what we are really looking for. If we are concerned with the causes of slumps—of a falling off in income from one year to the next—we want to know how consumption (or saving) responds when income *suddenly* changes. Here there is a different story to tell. In detail, it is complicated and still inconclusive—though the subject has been very much studied—but its very general outline is reasonably clear. In the face of rapid, short-term, changes in income, the proportion which is saved does not remain constant; as income falls it tends to decrease, and as income expands it tends to rise. In the three depressed years 1932, 1933, and 1934, indeed, personal savings in the United States actually became negative; people drew upon their savings to maintain their expenditure on consumption at a higher level than their current income.

What can be said more positively is that, in any economy, there is a general tendency for any increase or decrease in income to be followed by an increase or decrease in expenditure on consumers' goods which is a reasonably constant fraction of it. While, therefore, consumption expenditure as a whole is by no means a constant proportion of income as a whole, changes in consumption expenditure are in reasonably constant proportion to changes in income. In the United Kingdom, for instance, private expenditure on consumption, measured at the prices ruling in 1938, changed from year to year between 1929 and 1948 by about four-fifths of the corresponding changes in private income available after paying tax (similarly measured) except during the war years. In the United States, expenditure on consumption in the period 1929-40 changed from year to year by about 0·85 of the corresponding changes in personal income. The ratio of *total* consumption expenditure to *total* available income varied, however, in both countries during the period concerned; in 1929, private persons in the United States saved about 7 per cent. of their disposable income; in 1932, with incomes much lower, their expenditure exceeded their disposable income by about 2½ per cent.

So long as it is still true that the *changes* in consumption in a country are in a constant proportion to the *changes* in its national income, we can still deduce very easily a precise relation between changes in its investment and changes in its income—though the relation between its total investment and its total income is a little more complicated. If a change in income always brings a change (say) four-fifths as great in consumption expenditure (or one-fifth as great in saving), then any change in investment will bring a change in income five times as great. The ratio of change in consumption to change in income has come to be known as *the marginal propensity to consume* (it is four-fifths in this example), the ratio of change in saving to change in income (here one-fifth) as the *marginal propensity to save,* and the ratio of the change in income to the change in investment which causes it (here five) as *the multiplier.* In a simplified example such as we have taken, in which we can ignore foreign trade and public finance, the multiplier is always the inverse of the marginal propensity to save.

In practice, of course, economies are not as simple as that. Money leaks out of active circulation not only through saving, but also, as we have noted, by being spent on imports, and (we must add) by being taken by the tax-collector. The marginal propensity to save does not, therefore, adequately measure the proportion of any increase in income which (temporarily, at any rate) leaks away; to it we have to add a marginal propensity to import and (if the slightly comical flavour of the term may be excused) a 'marginal propensity to pay taxes'. We assume that the proportion of any additional income which 'leaks away' in the ways in question is constant. The sum of these three marginal propensities gives the proportion of any change in income which is *not* immediately passed on as a change in spending on consumption. Its inverse is now the multiplier. But what does this new multiplier multiply? Not simply changes in expenditure on investment goods, but also changes in those other classes of spending on the goods and services produced in the economy which are not already included in consumers' expenditure; namely, exports (i.e. foreign spending on the economy's products) and internal public expenditure. All these kinds of expenditure together we may class as 'non-consumption expenditure'. It is the change in this aggregate to which we have to apply the multiplier in order to deduce the consequential change in income.

If, then, we really can justifiably assume that consumption varies in a simple way with income, we are enabled to concentrate our attention on the other components of income—the components of 'non-consumption expenditure'—in seeking to explain changes which come about in the income level. In fact, consumption does not in all circumstances behave in the way here assumed. During the war, most notably, the shortage of consumers' goods, and the measures taken to ration them and to control their prices meant that expenditure on them sank, or stayed, far below the level which would have been expected from its peace-time relation to income— as much as 15 per cent. below in the United States, and 20 per cent. in the United Kingdom, for instance. After the war, too, when clothing, furniture, motor cars, and household equipment again became plentiful, the desire to re-equip with them, coupled with the existence of wartime savings with which they could be bought, meant that consumption expenditure for a time was somewhat higher in relation to income than pre-war experience would have indicated. In interpreting changes which have taken place in the level of economic activity, it is always wise to look at consumers' expenditure, and to see whether any special circumstance has made it deviate from its 'normal' relation to income; but the income-consumption relationship is nevertheless sufficiently steady in most countries and over most fairly short periods for the assumption that there *is* a 'normal' relationship to be a useful one; we have no need to try to explain all of the (usually relatively large) variation in consumption; we need only look at any 'abnormal' element which we may find in it, and can then proceed to scrutinize the various components of non-consumption expenditure.

Some case-studies in Depression
In order to show how economists set out to do this, it may be useful to take some historical examples. The slump which immediately springs to mind, because it is not only the most serious on record, but also the only big one for which we have reasonably good statistics, is the great slump of the early nineteen-thirties, especially as experienced in the United States. Between 1929 and 1933, the money value of the national income in that country fell by nearly half, the volume of industrial production by 40 per cent. and the level of real income by perhaps a quarter, while the number of

unemployed rose by something like twelve million. How can we begin to analyse this catastrophe?

In the first place, we may note that private expenditure on consumers' goods changed from year to year during the main slump years 1929-32 by very nearly a constant proportion—80 or 90 per cent.—of the corresponding year to year changes in personal incomes available after tax. Much the same, indeed, happened during the subsequent recovery, up to the outbreak of war. We can therefore conclude that consumers' expenditure was influenced mainly by changes in their available income, and that there is little reason to suppose that any independent changes in this expenditure, not attributable to income changes, was sufficient to make much difference to the course which income followed.

Secondly, we may ask how far personal incomes available for expenditure were maintained or diminished by changes in taxation, or in the public authorities' payments to persons for relief or other purposes other than current production. It is clear that tax payments fell off during the slump, but since the fall was only about $2\frac{1}{2}$ per cent. of the amount by which gross national product fell, it was not very important in this connection. The increase in transfer payments by the public authorities to persons between 1929 and 1933 was only about half as great as the fall in personal tax payments, so that, though it helped to maintain spending power, it was not very important either.

Thirdly, how far did purchasing power leak abroad? Changes in expenditure on goods and services from abroad during the slump were parallel with the fall in income, and were equal to about 8 per cent. of it. In so far as we can regard the fall in purchases from abroad as a *consequence* of the fall in income—not as something due to other causes—we may say that the 'marginal propensity to import' was about 0·08. In fact, there is reason to believe that some of the reduction in imports was due, not to the fall in income, but to the tariff increases introduced in 1930; but it will do no harm for the present purpose if we regard the whole of the reduction in payments abroad as consequent upon the American slump, and as a factor diminishing its severity by reducing the size of the multiplier.

If we do this, we must look on the fall in payments received by the United States for its exports of goods and services as part of the fall in non-consumption expenditure to which the multiplier has to be applied. This fall in receipts from abroad was about 4·8 billion dollars, or some 10 per cent. of the total fall in gross national product between 1929 and 1933. We must regard it as having made a substantial contribution to the slump—though some of it was certainly due to a fall in foreign incomes, of which the American slump was itself a substantial cause.[1]

We come now to the course of internal investment, and it at once becomes plain that the change in this was the major immediate cause of the slump. The fall in it between 1929 and 1933 was about 36 per cent. of the corresponding fall in gross national product. Moreover, nearly three-quarters of the change in investment within the country was due to fixed investment, as distinct from inventory investment, even though the change in the latter (equal to about 5 per cent. of the 1929 gross national product) were probably the largest, in relation to income, which have ever been recorded. So far as fixed investment is concerned, the biggest reductions both proportionately and absolutely were in building—house-building actually fell by nine-tenths—but purchases of industrial equipment fell heavily, too, and expenditure on fixed investment as a whole in 1933 was only a fifth of what it had been in 1929. To explain this fall would be, in effect, to carry the explanation of the great American depression a stage further, and it will be convenient to postpone this task until a little later.

The fall of inventory investment played, as we have seen, a smaller total part in the events of these years, but its part was still not negligible, and the course of inventory investment in a slump is always interesting. Broadly speaking, either of two things may happen; people who hold stocks of finished goods, semi-manufactured articles, or raw materials may decide that their stocks are too high in relation to current or expected sales, and may reduce their orders, thus causing a fall in income, or (usually because income has already fallen), purchases may fall and sellers thus find that the stocks on their hands are piling up. In the latter event, stockholders are likely then to reduce their orders vigorously and thus make a substantial contribution to the further reduction of income. To put it in another way, reductions in deliveries to stockholders may be reduced faster than their sales fall, thus bringing about a

---

[1] If we take the alternative view that changes in imports and exports are both to be regarded as outside events which contribute to the slump but do not result from it, we cannot regard the marginal propensity to import as something which enters into the calculation of the multiplier, and diminishes its value. We can, on the other hand, regard the *net* gain (if any) of purchasing power in transactions with the outside world as part of the non-consumption expenditure to changes in which the (larger) multiplier has to be applied. In fact, the net annual gain of purchasing power from the outside world diminished by only about half a billion dollars during the slump; foreign transactions therefore made a very small net contribution to the course of events in the United States.

reduction in their inventories, or they may not be reduced fast enough to match the fall in sales, so that inventories rise—but the latter state of affairs can hardly go on for long; reductions in orders for goods to be held in stock may be expected to become more drastic until they bring down actual inventories held into line with the reduced rate of sale.

In the United States there was some accumulation of inventories in the year 1929; probably a good deal of it was involuntary, since sales declined rather sharply in the later part of the year. During 1930, retailers managed to bring about a considerable reduction in their inventories, but wholesalers experienced a slight increase in theirs, and manufacturers' inventories were still piling up quite fast. It was only in 1931 that reduction in inventories became general, and only in the following year that it reached its maximum rate. We can conclude that, while inventory-holders were fairly quick in reducing their orders so as to keep, or to get, their inventories down, it was at the start a reduction in sales which called for reduction in orders rather than a move to reduce inventories which led to a fall in income and sales. Inventory reductions in a slump are bound to intensify it, but in the great American slump they do not seem either to have initiated it or to have been directly responsible for the greater part of it. The blame remains with fixed investment.

To see whether this is always so, let us look at three American slumps which have happened since—in 1937-8, 1948-9, and 1953-4. All these slumps—or, since they were all relatively mild in their consequences, these 'recessions'—had one feature in common; namely, that the fall in the rate of inventory investment (in all cases a change from net accumulation to net depletion of stocks) was large in relation to the fall in fixed investment. It was nearly twice as great as the fall in fixed investment in 1937-8, four times as great in 1948-9, and many times as great (since fixed investment hardly fell at all) in 1953-4. Such episodes (there had been others in the nineteen-twenties) have been well named 'inventory recessions'. It is clear that inventory investment is particularly liable to sudden changes of this kind, amounting to anything up to 5 per cent. of annual income.

Changes in inventory accumulation were, however, not the only changes in non-consumption expenditure in the instances just mentioned. In 1937-8, as we have just noted, fixed investment also fell, though only by about a fifth (the fall was mostly in purchases of industrial equipment). On the other side of the scale, there was some increase in public and social insurance relief payments and benefits; the recession was mild outside the United States so that there was very little fall in receipts from abroad; and there was perhaps a greater fall in leakage of purchasing power through imports than one would normally expect to follow from the 6 per cent. fall in income which actually occurred. It was perhaps more significant that government purchases of goods and services increased, in continuation of a trend which began in 1934. All the main elements in non-consumption expenditure except private investment within the country thus moved in such a way as to moderate the recession, whereas in the early 'thirties government purchases and net receipts of purchasing power from abroad had fallen.

The next recession, that of 1948-9, was still smaller in its ultimate scale—gross national product fell (in money value) by only some 2 per cent. though inventory investment declined by nearly twice as much; nearly as big a fall in relation to income as in 1929-32. On this occasion, fixed investment (as we have noted) fell very little, and though there was a falling off in exports (due to a combination of recovering production and dollar shortage in the outside world), this may perhaps be regarded as the nearest approach to a purely inventory recession among those we are discussing. The relatively small extent of the fall in gross national product is to be attributed to two things—a rise in government purchases which was equal to about 70 per cent. of the fall in inventory investment, and the curious behaviour of consumers, who increased their purchases in spite of a slight fall (made slight partly by a reduction in taxation) in their disposable income. A considerable part of the increase in government purchases was on account of defence—this was the time of the Berlin blockade and the accompanying increase of international tension. The increase in consumers' expenditure is to be attributed to the fact that households had still not raised their stocks of many things which had been scarce during and just after the war to the level which their income warranted. They had, indeed, refilled their wardrobes—spending on clothing decreased sharply—but supplies of motor cars, television equipment, and many other things were increasing, and were still less than people were willing to take up.

The recession of 1953-4 presents us with what looks, at first sight like still more striking anomalies, in that, though gross national product fell by just over 1 per cent. disposable personal income rose, and personal expenditure on consumption rose still more. This was an inventory recession only incidentally; the main reduction was in government expenditure on defence, as the Korean war ended. With this went a remission of taxation which accounts for the rise in disposable personal income. That the rise in consumption was greater still is less easy to explain, but some part at least of the explanation may be that in one important respect shortage attributable to the

M

world war and the pre-war depression was still not removed—
increased housing was still in great demand, and there was a big
increase in expenditure on rent. The importance of housing in the
events of the time is emphasized by the fact that building increased
during this short recession to an extent which almost offset the fall
in purchases of producers' equipment.

These examples have all been drawn from the United States,
partly because of the importance of that country in the world
economy, partly because of the wealth of information available
about economic changes there. If we look at events in most other
economies—such as the British—one difference which is to be
expected is the greater importance of the impact on the outside
world. Between 1929 and 1932, the British gross product fell in value
by some £650 million, or 13 per cent.—not much more than a third
of the percentage by which American income fell. Private consumption expenditure seems to have fallen by less than half of this—just
over £300 million—and there is no reason to suppose that causes
other than the reduction in income were important in governing
the fall. The public authorities did little to mitigate or accentuate
the change in private incomes; direct taxation rose between 1928-9
and 1931-2 by about £60 million, and so did transfer incomes, so
that the two changes offset each other. Public purchases of goods
and services were virtually unchanged. The tradition that public
finance should be neutral in this respect could hardly have made a
more dignified exit. Even gross private fixed investment expenditure
in the country seems to have fallen only by some £90 million, or
about a seventh, which is to be compared with the American four-
fifths. As to inventory investment, there is very little information
available, but it seems clear that inventories were already falling in
1929; it is likely that deliberate accumulation came to an end in
1928, and was succeeded by deliberate reduction, the change in this
type of investment from 1928 to 1930 being considerably over £100
million, or perhaps half as large in relation to income as the con-
temporary American change. Altogether, internal investment, fixed
and inventory, probably fell, however, by less than £200 million.

But exports and net receipts for services rendered abroad fell by
nearly £600 million. On the other hand expenditure on imports fell
by £400 million. Some of this reduction, of course, came about as
a consequence of the fall in British national income. How much we
cannot precisely say; it seems unlikely, however, that a 13 per cent.
fall in income would have caused a very big proportion of a 37 per
cent. fall in import expenditure by itself. Tariffs and, far more, a 30
per cent. fall in import prices—due partly to falling British demand,

but much more to falling demand in the United States and else-where—may be held responsible for most of the saving in the British import bill. It is, at any rate, clear that the fall in receipts from exports was at least three times as large as the fall in internal investment, and that the contra-item which can be taken as a determinant of the size of the income fall in this country, not a con-sequence of it—namely, the part of the fall in the import bill which was not due simply to the reduction of British incomes—was probably much greater than the fall in internal investment also. This is a measure of the extent to which, in the last great depression, the United Kingdom's fortunes were governed by external forces—which fortunately to a large measure offset each other. An even greater predominance of external causes over internal ones would be found if we studied the onset of depression in some of the still more 'open' economies, such as the Netherlands, Denmark, or New Zealand.

Since the war, the United Kingdom has so far suffered nothing that could be called a slump, and hardly anything that could be called a recession. Perhaps the main reason for this—in the light of what has just been said about the importance of external causes in the nineteen-thirties—is the almost steady increase in the volume of world trade since the war; an increase which was interrupted only by a very slight fall from 1951 to 1952. Fixed investment within the United Kingdom has shown an even steadier increase. The only important sources of disturbance have been changes in inventory investment, which have been accompanied, in general, by changes in the same direction in the buying habits of consumers. Thus, in 1947, 1951, and 1955 there were large accumulations of inventories accompanied by tendencies for consumers to spend more on goods, in relation to their available incomes, than in 'average' years. In some other years, but most notably in 1952, there was a depletion of inventories and, at the same time, a tendency for consumers to spend relatively little in relation to the incomes they had available after paying their direct taxes.

These variations in inventory investment and consumers' habits have been large enough, in themselves, to engender very considerable changes in the level of economic activity. That they have not had this effect (except to a minor extent in 1951-2) is due mainly to two causes. First, at least half of each increase and decrease in inventory investment has been accurately reflected in an increase or decrease of imports, so that only the remainder has constituted an increase or decrease in the demand for home-produced goods. Secondly, the very substantial fall in this demand associated with the inventory disinvestment of 1952 was largely offset by an increase in government spending on defence, and the method by which the government has financed its expenditure—its budgetary policy—has on the whole, worked in a stabilizing direction. It is clear, however, that these stabilizing factors would not have been adequate if we had been faced with a fall in demand for our exports on anything like the scale of that in 1929-32.

Causes and Interactions

We have now looked at some slumps which seem to have had different principal causes—shrinkages in internal fixed investment, inventory investment, government spending, or purchases by the outside world. We have not, however, yet taken the enquiry any further by considering the causes of the shrinkages in question, nor have we discussed ways in which one of these shrinkages may operate to produce another. In doing this, we may leave changes in government purchase of goods and services aside, since the cause is often obvious and often political. In the future we may see certain kinds of public investment varied for economic reasons, in order to stabilize the level of activity, but there have been few instances so far in which this was the dominant motive. Again, we need not say much about shrinkage of exports, which is normally the result either of depression in some other part of the world, of trade barriers, or of a shift in demand such as we discussed at the beginning of this chapter.

This leaves us with private internal investment, either fixed or inventory. The possible reasons why fixed investment should fall from time to time are numerous. Theorists have argued that, since the extension of capital is undertaken to provide for an increase of income, investment will fall whenever the expected rate of increase of income (which may often be geared to the current rate of increase of income) is reduced. Others have argued that businessmen are less subtle than this—that they invest when times are good and cease to invest when times become bad; the badness of the time consisting in (or being signalled to them by) either a low level of sales or a low level of profits. Again, it has been argued that, especially where the investment is in long-lived capital equipment, like houses, railways or ships, a very sensitive adjustment of it to demand for the equipment in question would be required to prevent quite large discrepancies between the amount in existence and the amount required, and that these would lead to both rushes to stock up and pauses when the stock had become excessive. We have seen in the discussion of the price mechanism (Chapter 5) that a sensitive and prompt adjustment of this kind may be made unlikely by the mere existence of a time-lag between the making of decisions to produce (to invest in this case) and the completion of the product. Variations in monetary conditions are also claimed to influence the rate of fixed investment.

The large amount of extremely difficult statistical analysis which has been undertaken in the last twenty or thirty years gives some support to all these suggestions, but with great differences in emphasis according to the period and the country investigated, and nearly always with a good deal of ambiguity.

Inventory investment is more fickle than fixed investment; orders for most of the things which manufacturers and traders keep in stock are repeated or adjusted rather frequently, and are easily changed from one month to the next. The sizes of inventories which people want to hold are presumably related to expected sales and to expected price-changes—if prices are expected to rise, inventories will be laid in quickly, and if they are expected to fall inventories will be run down so as to postpone new purchases, if possible until the goods have cheapened. If sales are expected to increase, bigger inventories will be wanted, so that orders will be increased by rather more than the expected increase in sales; if sales are expected to fall, there will probably be a desire to decrease inventories, with the result that orders may be cut back heavily. Moreover, if sales decrease unexpectedly, inventories are as we have seen left higher than normal, so that an especially heavy cut in orders is likely to follow, particularly if the fall in sales is expected to continue. The fickleness of inventory investment is not hard to account for.

It follows from what has been said about the causes of variation in the two kinds of internal investment that any change (say a fall) in either of them is likely to react both upon the other and upon itself, in such a way that the fall is reinforced. A fall in inventory investment, for instance, leads to a fall in production of goods, and so a fall in income; this reduces sales of goods and thus leads to unexpected and unwanted inventory accumulation, which will cause orders for goods to be reduced still more. The fall in income is quite likely, also, to lead to a downward revision of plans for fixed investment, which, when it takes effect, will reduce income still further. Similarly, any fall in fixed investment, by reducing income and sales, not only will almost certainly cause a net reduction of inventories (perhaps after an initial, unwanted, accumulation of them) but may also cause fixed investment plans to be further cut.

These interactions and the order in which they occur can sometimes be discerned. In the United States after 1929, for instance, the slump came primarily from a fall in fixed investment and the fall in inventory investment, though it reinforced it, played a subsidiary and somewhat delayed part (involuntary stock accumulation in the later part of 1929 was a sign that sales of consumers' goods were falling ahead of production). The great fall in fixed investment was, like others of its kind, self-reinforcing; it went on largely because it had started; but from its beginning it was strengthened by special circumstances. For one thing, the enormous stock-exchange collapse, beginning in the autumn of 1929, undermined confidence in the health of the economy generally; for another, it seems that, in the nineteen-twenties, much investment had been connected with the re-shaping of American life to a pattern made possible by the invention of the motor car, and that when this re-shaping was completed, no stimulus of comparable power presented itself for some time. Some inventions possess this power of instigating widespread changes which require heavy investment—in this case in new suburbs, roads, and the petroleum industry, as well as in the manufacture and servicing of motor vehicles themselves. There is no reason to expect the supply of such inventions to be steady and regular. Their irregularity is an independent source of hazard in economic life.

In the United Kingdom at the same time, as we have seen, the slump came mainly from abroad, but a reduction in inventory investment began in 1928, before the fall in home fixed investment, though not necessarily before the decisions which led to it. Reduction of inventories seems to have played a considerably bigger relative (though not absolute) part in the great slump in the United Kingdom than it did in the United States and has some claim to have been an independent cause, not simply a consequence of a decline in income already begun.

In the remaining slumps, or recessions, which we looked at earlier in this chapter, it was remarkable that fixed investment did not fall very far; with the exception of the recession of 1953-4, when government purchases fell more than inventory investment, they remained substantially 'inventory recessions'. Why was this? In 1938 it was probably due largely to the low level to which the stock of fixed capital had sunk. Investment by business had, ever since 1930, been insufficient to cover the ordinary maintenance and depreciation of firms' fixed equipment, which meant that, unless income was actually falling, the equipment was bound eventually to become patently insufficient to meet the demand for its services. Income— and therefore total demand for goods and services—had been rising since 1933 (apart from the setback in 1937-8), in spite of the low absolute rate of gross investment. The case which would present itself to businessmen for extending (or perhaps still more for modernizing) their equipment must therefore have been growing stronger, and the case for reducing investment even in a time of recession must have been much weaker than it had been in, say, 1930.

This consideration throws some light on the answer to a question which has probably occurred to the reader already—if falls in investment and income tend to be self-reinforcing (as we have argued), why do they ever come to an end? It may be that, if the rate of replacement and extension of fixed capital sinks low, the stock will slowly fall in relation to the calls upon it, and will become more and more old-fashioned in relation to the current technical possibilities. This is the counterpart of one of the possible reasons given above for a decline in fixed investment—namely, that if it has been at a high level, the stock of capital may have grown out of proportion to the demands upon it. The shortage of capital equipment of at least some kinds in relation to income was probably a strong reason for a limited nature of the recession not only in 1937-8 but in 1948-9, 1953-4, and other mainly 'inventory' recessions as well; housing in particular remained for many years after the war inadequate in relation to the greatly raised level of American real incomes and the increased number of families. It is only in some inventory recessions, not by any means all, that plans for fixed investment are likely to be sensitive to a fall in the level of income.

Moreover, unless it precipitates a fall in fixed investment, an inventory recession seems likely to be short, if sharp. It normally involves a transition from accumulation of inventories to quite rapid depletion, and such depletion brings manufacturers' and dealers' stocks down in relation to their actual and expected sales. The point is thus bound to be reached where inventories stand at what are regarded as the proper level, or even too low a level, and orders are then again raised. There is a 'floor' below which stocks cannot be allowed to sink, just as there is a limit to the disinvestment of fixed capital.

These considerations may suggest something of the possible mechanisms by which falls in the level of activity and of income may be brought to a halt. It would not be appropriate to pursue them further here; nor need we extend the discussion of slumps into a systematic treatment of the 'trade cycle'—the supposedly regular alternation of increases and decreases in activity—with which they are generally associated. It is true that, for at least half a century before the first world war, and with some reservation, between the two world wars, fluctuations in economic activity in the principal advanced countries showed a good deal of regularity. In most such countries there was a cycle averaging eight or nine years from one slump to the next, which seems to be associated mainly with fluctuation in fixed investment. In some of them, most notably the United States, there is to be seen superimposed on this a fluctuation which is apparently connected mainly with inventory investment—a cycle reckoned to average forty months from one downturn to another.

The reader may observe a continuation of this 'short cycle' in the post-war American inventory recessions to which we have referred —1948 and 1953, and that of 1957-8 which is still proceeding as these words are written. But an intermediate one is called for to preserve the tradition. In fact, there are traces of one in 1951-2. The heavy accumulation of stocks in 1950-51, at the time when the Korean war first broke out and then threatened to spread, was followed by a period of much slower growth. But the rapid expansion of armament expenditure, if nothing else, swamped any tendency to recession in general activity which this might otherwise have caused. Moreover, many European countries experienced a recession in 1951-2, and another beginning in 1957, and in the United Kingdom the variations in inventories, which have already been referred to, can be regarded as constituting a 'cycle' which, however, has been largely masked by other influences. Since 1939 there is no trace to be seen of the eight- or nine-year cycle in fixed investment in any country.

The theoretical treatment of both these cycles, as regular and systematic phenomena, has been a major industry among economists, and some of the results possess great interest and elegance, which should commend them to all serious students of the subject. But for the purpose of this introductory sketch of the world economy, it may suffice to regard slumps rather than cycles as matters of practical concern. Inventory slumps, whether regular or not, are clearly still with us. Slumps in fixed investment, notwithstanding our twenty-year freedom from them, should be regarded as a very real possibility especially as the various economies of the world wipe off the enormous arrears of development attributable to the war and the depression years before it. There is increased apprehension of this in the spring of 1958. Far greater awareness of the danger and far greater powers of dealing with it than have existed before are now to be found though in varying degrees in the main centres in which it could arise; but the powers are still untried, and the adequacy of the determination to use them is in some important cases open to question.

The Hazards of Inflation

This suggests a final point. It is commonplace that wartime and post-war discussion of economic reconstruction were overshadowed by the fear of depression, and that the practical problem which has emerged has been not depression but inflation. Inflation has not so far been included among the hazards of economic life in this chapter, but a hazard it certainly is, for any person or community with an income wholly or partly fixed in money value; a broad category, which includes international creditor countries like the United States, all those persons who receive pensions or interest on bonds, and those wage and salary earners whose rates of pay are revised infrequently or not sufficiently generously to match the cost of living.

Inflation, like depression, is subject to many variations, but the most important distinction to make in this connection is that between its working in an economy where prices are flexible and its working in one where they are in some sense 'administered'. We have discussed some aspects of this distinction already in Chapter 5. Where prices are entirely flexible in the sense that they are determined from day to day by supply and demand in the market, inflation is brought about by causes which are the simple opposite of those which bring about a slump—that is to say, by an increase in purchasing power in active circulation beyond the point where such an increase cannot simply call forth a greater volume of production—perhaps because one or more factors of production are fully employed. If we assume, as before, that consumption stands throughout in a simple relation to income, we may regard inflation of this kind as due to an excess of non-consumptive expenditure, which may be due primarily to heavy government expenditure, heavy exports, or heavy private expenditure on investment goods. Examples, though imperfect ones, may be found in a number of countries in the early years of the second world war, where price control was not yet effective—in the United States up to 1941, for instance (though few factors were fully employed by then), in Hungary up to 1943, as well as in India and a number of countries in the Middle East.

In such an inflation, where the free market prices of finished goods and services are raised by pressure of spending, one might expect that profits would increase more than other shares of the national income, and that the real incomes of wage-earners and receivers of salaries, rents, and interest would therefore tend to fall. In recent experience, real wages generally seem to have been rather well maintained during inflations even where prices were most flexible; at all events the share which wage-earners could claim in the national income has seldom fallen, even though the share which went to profits may have fared better still. Salaries and (still more) rents, pensions, and interest have usually fared worst, simply because they were least frequently revised. An inflationary situation which raises prices in the free market also raises wages in the free market, if they are determined in one, or, if they are not, does at all events make organized labour acutely conscious of the desirability of keeping up with the rising cost of living, and gives it a favourable situation in which to bargain for the purpose.

Where prices of finished goods and services are fixed by producers on the basis of cost of production, the initiative in raising them will appear to come from the prices of factors of production. If these are flexible, and are fixed in a free market, then any excessive rise in them will seem to be attributable to an excessive pressure of demand in the economy, and will, again, be removable by reducing government spending, exports, and private investment in the country. Matters are not, however, always so easy. In Chapter 5 it has been remarked that wages and salaries are not very sensitive to reductions in demand in most modern economies, and that the prices of primary products, while they are sensitive to world demand, are not easily prevented from rising by a limitation of demand in any one country acting alone—unless that country is the United States. Most advanced western countries, therefore, are liable to encounter sources of inflation which they cannot easily combat by policies aimed at reducing spending. One of these sources is a rise in the prices of imports, caused by a heavy world demand for them (if they are primary products) or rising costs of production (if they are manufactured goods). The other is a rise in the country's own wage or salary rates, attributable to the general nature of its bargaining machinery, which makes a curbing of the rise by reduction in total demand ineffective, unless it is so drastic as to be socially unacceptable.

Where either of these sources of inflation is the main one, it seems still to be true that the main victims are the receivers of pensions, interest, and rent. Inflation of this kind is serious precisely because both wage-earners and profit-receivers are in a position to protect their interests. It is the rest of the community, therefore (with salary earners usually in an intermediate position) which suffers. It is true that, where the inflation originates from a rise in import prices, real wages are liable to be reduced—because there is some delay before money wages catch up to the rise in the cost of living consequent upon dearer imports. It is also true that, where particularly aggressive and successful bargaining for higher wages is the initiating cause of the inflation, the share of wages in the total income will be slightly increased, because prices and profits lag some way behind. But experience suggests that these are generally only rather small changes in relation to the loss suffered by those who are neither wage nor profit receivers, or those who hold (for them) substantial assets of fixed money value. It is no doubt because the hazards of inflation are largely limited to a minority of the population that it has been found, in moderation, to be a tolerable process.

Inflation can, however, go beyond the bounds of moderation and become a hazard to a whole economy, in as much as it can deprive it of many of the practical advantages which flow from possessing a monetary system. When prices are generally expected to go on rising at more than a moderate rate then not only do they rise extremely fast by reason of that very expectation, but the expectation makes people avoid holding money whenever they can, even at the cost of a good deal of inconvenience. Moreover, since the future course of prices becomes unpredictable (apart from the presumption that they will rise), money becomes an unsuitable unit in which to demand future payment, and bargains begin to be made in terms of cigarettes or glasses of beer. A modern economy cannot work smoothly on this basis, and it becomes necessary in such cases virtually to scrap the existing monetary units and start again. Germany had to do this in 1923, Greece in 1944, and Hungary in 1946.

'Hyper-inflation' of this kind is, however, not a common phenomenon. It has not happened in modern times in any country which was not disorganized by foreign invasion or occupation, and it should be regarded as a hazard of a very different order from those by which most western countries have been faced in recent years.

CHAPTER 12

The Organization of the World Economy

THE foregoing chapters have, it is hoped, given the reader some idea of the general nature of the world economy, and of a few of the problems to which its structure and working give rise. In brief, it can be regarded as a collection of national economies, differing from one another enormously in their sizes, occupational structures, modes of organization, the average livings which they provide for the people in them, and the extent to which their economic lives are bound up with the rest of the world. These differences arise partly from the facts of physical and political geography and of population distribution, but even more, perhaps, from differences in level of development—in the possession and application to production of knowledge, enterprise, organizing power, and capital equipment. Partly for this reason, and partly because of the continual advance of the frontiers of technical knowledge and the changes in consumers' tastes and governments' policies, the pattern of economic activity as a whole, especially the pattern and the terms of transactions between different national economies, is in constant flux. Moreover, in addition to the advance of productive power, which goes on in different economies at such diverse rates, and with such considerable differences in the nature of the products, there is variation—sometimes very sharp variation—in the extent to which the existing productive capacity is actually used.

In addition to the slight explorations which have been attempted earlier in the book of these matters separately, is there anything to be said about the organization of world, or international, economic activity as a whole? Are there any attempts to promote development and control the hazards of the world's economic life through international institutions?

The End of laissez faire
Three or four generations ago, many people would have answered these questions by saying that the world did, indeed, seem to be evolving quite rapidly towards a single principle of organization, though one which did not demand conscious control of any important aspect of the whole world economy—it seemed to be

evolving towards a single market economy. The main countries had, in effect, already got a single monetary system based upon gold. It seemed that there was a trend towards free trade in goods, so that the gold price of any kind of product might be expected to become the same all over the world, apart from differences which could be attributed to transport costs (which were themselves falling). Even the factors of production capital and labour seemed to be becoming more mobile internationally. It might have seemed that savings in any country would soon be distributed between investments in different parts of the world according to their prospective returns, as freely as between enterprises in the savers' own country. Indeed, the United Kingdom was already reaching this state of affairs. A corresponding degree of international mobility of labour can hardly have seemed a near prospect, in spite of the large scale of European migration to the New World, but it looked as if the world was rapidly becoming a single market for transportable goods and for capital; a market in which the total supplies, prices and destinations of these commodities would be determined by the mechanism of free markets.

Moreover, it would have been very widely accepted that this result would be eminently satisfactory. Although recurrent depressions were familiar, they were not regarded as demanding any major reform of, or interference with, the free market system—there was, indeed, no generally accepted explanation of them at all. The distribution of capital between industries and economies through a free market was also thought to be the best distribution that could be devised; to leave economic development to the judgement of investors, who had the strongest motives for judging well, seemed to be the best way of placing capital where it would increase world income to the greatest possible extent.

Although, as has been remarked in Chapter 10, there were some important moves away from free trade in goods from the eighteen-seventies onwards, and though freedom of trade and of international capital movements never became anything like complete, this picture of world activity and development as regulated only by the impersonal forces of free markets may be said to have remained reasonably true until the first world war. Indeed, when after that war it became necessary to take some conscious decisions about the re-establishment of national and international practices and institutions relating to trade and money, most people concerned paid at least lip-service to the ideal of a free-trade unregulated world economy with gold as, in effect, the world-wide monetary substance. How, and how far, have the relevant facts and aspirations moved away from this?

Although the first world war was no doubt the original cause of a good many of the changes which subsequently happened, it was with the great depression of the early nineteen-thirties that the old picture of world economy's organization ceased to be valid either as even an approximate representation of its true state, or for most people, as an ideal that it seemed possible to restore. In the first place, the depression was far bigger than any previous one. With thirty million unemployed in the principal industrial countries of the world, it was no longer plausible to regard depression as an acceptable price to be paid for a generally beneficent system. Its relation to the system demanded investigation. In the second place, the severity of the depression, coupled with the fact that governments had become, in the war, more accustomed than previously to intervening in economic life, produced a great crop of restrictions on imports. These were intended to increase employment in the countries that applied them, and would no doubt have done so if only a few countries had acted in this way—though at the expense of increased unemployment, due to diminished exports, in the countries that did not. Since they were so generally applied, however, they had very little employment-creating effect for any country; they deprived the world of some of the benefits of inter-national specialization and caused some additional unemployment by dislocating the pattern of trade and commerce.

The third great effect of this depression was the disruption of the world-wide monetary system based upon gold. When people who have hitherto held large amounts of any particular currency decide, for any reason, to give it up, this is bound to lower its price in relation to other currencies and to gold unless others are willing to take it up at the original price. If there is a net tendency on the part of all the holders of a currency, taken together, to want to get rid of it, the monetary authorities of the country concerned are left to do what they can to maintain its value by buying it up in this way. To do so, however, they must have adequate reserves of gold or of other currencies. At a fairly advanced stage in the depression of the nineteen-thirties, there was widespread loss of confidence in the ability of the authorities in the United Kingdom to do this; the resulting scramble to get rid of sterling brought about the very event anticipated—the forced abandonment of that currency's gold value. Developments of this kind are contagious; indeed, the lowering of the gold values of currencies was taken up as another means, rather like the imposition of import restrictions, of increasing demand for a country's goods at the expense of other countries. Those countries (notably in Central Europe) which kept their currencies at their old nominal gold value were able to do so only by making it impossible (or, at least, illegal) to exchange them freely for gold, or for other currencies. These countries were obliged, in order to carry on trade even at a reduced level, to enter into special agreements, some of them akin to barter, with each other and with countries in the rest of the world, and some opportunities of specialization and trade which demanded non-bilateral patterns of settlement were thus forfeited. As for the countries which devalued their currencies, since they all did it, there was in the end little or no lasting effect on the level of unemployment in most of them, except perhaps an adverse one which sprang from loss of confidence in foreign currencies, and so in foreign transactions. It would be wrong to imply that the collapse of the former world monetary system based upon gold had a cata-strophic effect; traders and governments showed great ingenuity in finding means to trade where trade was most advantageous; but the monetary confusion and uncertainty were, to say the least, unhelpful.

Fourthly, as we have already seen in Chapter 5, the depression years were the great period of schemes for maintaining or stabilizing the prices of commodities. International cartels (such as the Euro-pean steel cartel) also arose or increased in strength, their aim being to avoid competition in the prevailing conditions of depression by dividing markets by agreement between firms or between national industries. Such schemes presented obvious dangers and some at least potential advantages; but whatever their merits or demerits, it was clear that they constituted a new element in the world economy, at variance with the pattern towards which it might have been supposed to be developing fifty years before.

Finally, among the effects of the depression which have already been mentioned, there was the virtual cessation of international lending, which had played such a vital part in making possible the development of much of the world, and which has not yet even been resumed on anything like its old scale. On the other hand, inde-pendently of the depression, and slightly preceding it, there came the first Russian Five-Year Plan—which marked not only the first estab-lishment, in peacetime, of a fully production-planned large economy, but also the inauguration of a rapid industrialization carried out by central direction with an unprecedentedly low degree of dependence upon the outside world, and relying for such external contacts as it had upon state trading.

With all these developments, the world economy on the eve of the second world war clearly did not present the appearance, as it had done two generations earlier, of being on the way to becoming a single, smoothly-working market economy with little need for positive action by governments, either singly or in co-operation, to keep it working and growing well. It had been found to be subject to depressions of ruinous violence, for which economists were beginning to understand the proper remedial governmental action, but against which governments had taken a good deal of 'beggar-my-neighbour' action, successful only in making matters worse. International trade was reduced in volume, largely by artificial barriers, despite the recovery of production after the depression. There was no longer anything like a world-wide monetary system, nor an active international capital market. Governments had come into the game actively, whether as complete planners of production, development, and foreign trade, as in the Soviet Union, as promotors of recovery by their own spending, as in the United States, France, Germany, and Sweden, as restricters of production, as in the control schemes, or as diverters of demand from foreign to domestic products, as nearly everywhere. By their action, or lack of it, they were capable of frustrating each other's intentions, and producing chaos unless they worked in consultation with each other, or within the framework of some set of rules.

It was plain, then, that the world economy (as distinct from national economies) would present statesmen with a number of urgent tasks after the war, quite apart from the tasks connected immediately with the damage and dislocation which the war had caused. The most important of these tasks was, perhaps, to provide machinery for international consultation in economic matters, and, if possible, rules within which national policies could be conducted without stultifying each other—'beggar-my-neighbour' policies had, as far as possible, to be ruled out. More positively, it seemed necessary to take such international action as might help to prevent a repetition of the great depression of the 'thirties, to restore a more freely working world monetary system, to remove as far as possible the accumulated barriers to international trade, and either to restore or to find a substitute for international lending as an aid to development.

The United Nations Organization and its Agencies

Let us look, then, very briefly, at the machinery which has been set up to accomplish these tasks. First, there is the Economic and Social Council of the United Nations; nominally the central organ of consultation on economic and social affairs for the whole world. The word 'consultation' must be stressed. Just as the United Nations Organization in general is in no sense a world government with power to make or administer laws (though some of its members have taken joint action under its auspices on special occasions, as in the

Korean crisis of 1950 and the Suez crisis of 1956), so the Economic and Social Council cannot cause action to be taken, except in so far as its members not only agree on resolutions in it but choose to ratify them. So far, it has not achieved any important economic action, partly because, as we shall see, the matters on which the interests of governments are most closely bound together have been dealt with through the 'specialized agencies' of the United Nations, or (especially in so far as they were acute problems of readjustment arising out of the war), through special and less permanent organizations, like those connected with Marshall aid. The central economic machinery of the United Nations does, however, perform two important functions. In the first place, like the League of Nations before it, it possesses a secretariat which prepares regular reports and studies of the general working of the world economy. With the improved understanding in the last generation of the causes of variations in economic activity and of the lines of action that can be taken to control them, reports of this kind have become an invaluable basis for policy decisions by governments, whether they have adequate machinery for analysing the particular problems of their own countries economies or not. The same can be said of the reports prepared by the regional commissions of the United Nations —the Economic Commission for Europe, the Economic Commission for Latin America, and the Economic Commission for Asia and the Far East.

Secondly, the Economic and Social Council has been responsible (at least formally) for the appointment of independent expert committees to recommend measures for dealing with a number of the central problems of the world economy—the maintenance of full employment, the reduction of the international impact of recessions that may occur in any part of the world, the economic development of under-developed countries, and the provision of special funds for economic development. The reports of these groups of experts, between them, sketch lines of growth for international institutions and national economic policies which seem to be far more helpful and realistic than any which were thought out between the two world wars. They have not, unfortunately, yet resulted in any important positive action—the sense of urgency in international economic affairs in the nineteen-fifties has been insufficient and the preoccupation with the burdens imposed by the cold war too great. We shall, however, have to mention these proposals again later, since they amount in large part to suggestions for the further development of the Specialized Agencies, to which we must now turn.

N

The Specialized Agencies of the United Nations are the main institutions through which economic co-operation on a world-wide scale takes place. Some of them continue long-established traditions. The International Telecommunications Union, for instance, was founded (as the International Telegraph Union) in 1865, and the Universal Postal Union in 1874. These two organizations, as well as, for example, the newer International Civil Aviation Organization, are clearly concerned with matters on which some international understanding (on wave-lengths, international postage arrangements, airport and transit facilities, and so on) is vital to the operation of international services. Other agencies, such as the World Health Organization and the World Meteorological Organization, are concerned largely with the world-wide collection and international dissemination of information of urgent practical importance. All these agencies, and others, moreover, are now involved in the programmes of technical assistance, whereby experts on various technical and economic matters are sent at the request of member governments of the United Nations to advise them—the cost being borne either by the general budgets of the Organizations concerned, or by a special account to which member governments make voluntary contributions.

The Food and Agriculture Organization, which is essentially the international counterpart of the agricultural advisory and statistical services which most governments provide in their own territories, is especially heavily involved in the technical assistance programmes. So, in the fields of labour legislation, methods of training, and industrial relations, is the International Labour Organization, which began as the International Labour Office in 1920. The ILO, however, has also provided perhaps the most impressive example of the way in which an international organization can make moral pressure effective by persuading member governments to subscribe to, and ratify, a large number of conventions on conditions of work and related matters.

By far the most important of the specialized agencies so far as the general working of the world economy is concerned, however, are the International Monetary Fund and the International Bank for Reconstruction and Development. These two organizations, together with an International Trade Organization which failed to take shape, constituted the main attempt of governments to meet the international monetary and economic difficulties which emerged in the nineteen-thirties, and which were outlined in the first section of this chapter.

The Fund was intended to accomplish three main purposes. First it was meant to restore something like a world-wide monetary system by establishing agreed relative values for its members' currencies and promoting as rapidly as possible their free convertibility into one another. Secondly, it was meant to pledge members to alter these 'par values' of their currencies only within narrow limits or by agreement, and in any case only as and when necessary to restore balance between payments to and from the member country in question. Competitive devaluation like that of the nineteen-thirties was thus to be prevented. Thirdly, the Fund was intended to provide reserves of international purchasing-power for its members, so that any one of them could withstand a temporary fall, for example, in its export earnings without having to take hasty steps to cut down its imports. In this way it was hoped not only to avoid the setting up of trade barriers which might be difficult subsequently to remove, but to prevent a temporary fall in demand in any one country from spreading round the world, as the depression which had its main centres in the United States and Germany had spread into the nineteen-thirties.

The International Bank had simpler objects; it was intended to take the part which private international investment had formerly played in promoting development by borrowing where it could and lending to governments or other substantial borrowers for approved development schemes.

How far have these two important agencies succeeded? It must be admitted, that, so far, their success has been only partial. The aim of achieving interconvertibility of currencies, amounting in effect to a unified world monetary system, has, in the first place, been frustrated by the enormously strong and continuing tendency for the demand for goods and services from certain countries (notably the United States) to be in excess of those countries' demands for imports. This has meant that American dollars (and in some degree certain other currencies) have been scarce, and that other countries have not been able to undertake to supply them freely to anyone who wanted them in exchange for their own currencies. Moreover, the reserves of dollars and other scarce currencies possessed by the Fund have been totally inadequate to supply the deficiency. The rules of the Fund limit the rate at which all members together, except the United States, could draw dollars from it to about $1½ billion a year—at which rate of drawing its gold and dollar resources would last only a little over two years. But in the single year 1947 purchases of goods and services from the United States exceeded sales to the United States by over $11 billion. The average annual discrepancy over the whole post-war

N*

period has been two or three times as great as the total rate at which other members could have drawn U.S. dollars from the Fund, in spite of the limits which most countries actually placed upon purchases made with dollars.

It is plain, then, that the Fund could not have gone any substantial part of the way to enable its members to make the dollar purchases which they have actually made; still less could it have enabled them to make their currencies freely convertible into dollars, which would have involved their supplying many more dollars in exchange for their own currencies than they actually did. In fact, what enabled purchases from North America to proceed at the rate they did was Marshall (and subsequently other kinds of) Aid, which at its peak provided about $4 billion a year. Indeed, the Fund was never designed to take care of the immediate post-war unbalance of payments, and both the extent and the duration of that unbalance had, in any case, been grossly under-estimated. But, quite apart from the exceptional dislocation following the war, which was very well dealt with by the exceptional measures of American aid, it is plain that the Fund is far too small to cope with the temporary shortages of a particular currency which are liable to occur. Quite a small American recession might reduce the value of American imports by $3 or $4 billion in a year; it has been estimated that a major recession might leave a gap of something like $10 billion spread over two years. The dollar resources of the Fund could not help much in such a case. The fact is that it was designed at a time when the post-war value of all international trade seemed likely to be less than half of what it has now grown to; and the provision made was inadequate even on the assumptions of the time. The resources of the Fund require to be multiplied by a factor of at least five if it is to be enabled to do what was originally intended.

The Bank made a slow start, but has built up both confidence in the markets from which it borrows and a set of workable criteria to govern its lending. It is now responsible for something like a quarter of the annual international investment in the world—but, as we have seen, the world total is only about a third in real value of the corresponding total in the nineteen-twenties. Here, again, if the more ambitious intentions of the founders are to be realized, a large increase in scale is required. But how far the scale could be extended without lowering the standards of productiveness and 'soundness' of the projects which are financed below the level on which the Bank now insists is another question.

It has been mentioned that, along with the Fund and the Bank, it was originally intended to set up an International Trade

Organization, designed to set agreed limits to the circumstances in which trade barriers other than tariffs were employed (in brief, to confine them to the removal of temporary balance of payments deficits), and to promote negotiations for the reduction of tariffs also. The extremely elaborate Charter which was agreed for this purpose was, in the end, not ratified; instead, however, there was established a General Agreement on Tariffs and Trade—a rather less formal club of the main trading nations which, through it, have negotiated very considerable reductions in their trade barriers, and have agreed not to raise the existing, or new, barriers against a very large number of items—items which, in fact, seem to constitute nearly half of the international trade of the world. At one stage in the negotiations for the International Trade Organization, there was (as has been mentioned in Chapter 5) a hope in some quarters that a comprehensive series of schemes might eventually be set up to stabilize the prices of the main primary commodities. Out of this there have come a number of Commodity Study Groups and an Interim Co-ordinating Committee for International Commodity Agreements, but, as was explained earlier, the atmosphere has not been favourable to the establishment of control schemes.

Co-ordination in Europe

This, then, in very rough outline, is the principal machinery established under the United Nations Organization to help the working of the world economy. To it we must add the international machinery which has been established for, geographically, more limited tasks. By far the most important machinery of this kind is that which developed in Europe as a result mainly of the United States' offer, in 1947, of large-scale material help in European reconstruction on condition that the receiving countries co-operated with one another to achieve the greatest possible degree of efficiency in the use of their resources. The Organization for European Economic Co-operation was set up to bring this about.

The Organization was responsible, in the first place, for co-ordinating the recovery plans of the separate member countries on western Europe. What this co-ordination amounted to is hard to judge; national plans were the basis of the requirements for aid which were submitted to the United States, and the extent to which they were modified by the OEEC was probably, on the whole, not very great. The great accomplishments of the Organization have been essentially the same as those which the Specialized Agencies of the United Nations attempted on a larger scale—the provision of an international payments system and the reduction of trade barriers.

The payments system which finally emerged is the European Payments Union, which has been in operation since 1950. It is a system whereby the balance which each of the eighteen members owes to, or is owed by, all the others together is worked out each month by the Bank for International Settlements (an institution originally set up in 1930 to facilitate the payment of German reparations arising from the war of 1914-18). These balances owed or owing are partly paid to, or by, the Payments Union in gold or dollars, partly 'chalked up', though once the member's debt to the Union reaches a certain 'quota', he has to pay any additional trading debt in gold or dollars —he is allowed no further credit. What this means is that the OEEC countries have constructed for themselves a multilateral payments system, which is equivalent to having their currencies freely convertible into each other for purposes of trade, though they are not convertible into dollars. This, with dollars scarce in relation to practically all other currencies, was a very reasonable thing to do, even though it may seem to conflict with the ultimate objectives of the International Monetary Fund.

The freeing of intra-European trade from trade barriers has involved two operations—'liberalization', which in this context means removing barriers other than tariffs, and movements towards customs unions. 'Liberalization' was fairly rapid and successful. Movements towards customs unions have been slower. The most advanced of these unions is that between Belgium, Holland and Luxembourg, which was negotiated during the war, but it is not yet complete, and still presents severe problems. The other large scheme in this field, superseding a number of earlier proposals, is, of course, that for the European Economic Community—a complete customs union of France, Western Germany, Italy, and Benelux (the Belgian-Luxembourg-Netherlands Union) to be attained gradually over a period of fifteen years. To this community it is proposed that the United Kingdom and other OEEC countries should link themselves in a 'Free Trade Area' by gradually dismantling their tariff walls with the Community countries and with each other. This is an ambitious project, bristling with difficulties, which it is beyond the purpose of this book to discuss. What additional pieces of international economic machinery will prove necessary to make either the Community or the Free Trade Area work remains to be seen.

One other piece of machinery which has already emerged from the European effort at economic co-operation, however, is the Coal and Steel Community, which came into existence in 1953, to create a common market for coal and steel in the same six countries from which the European Economic Community is to be formed. The creation of a common market in this case means not only the abolition of all nationally-imposed trade barriers to the commodities in question, but the complete revision of transport charges on them, which had developed in such a way as to be highly discriminatory. This complicated task is entrusted to a supra-national body, appointed in the last analysis by the legislatures of the six countries.

These European achievements and projects are, of course, important in changing the face of the world economy, and as experiments in or examples of the partial merging of national sovereignty in economic matters. But it is important to remember that they are restricted in scope, not only geographically but in the matters to which they pertain. European free trade has not been linked with proposals for the maintenance of full employment, or the joint financing of development. For this there are at least partly adequate reasons. The countries concerned remain part of a wider world economy, in which, even collectively, they are responsible for less than a quarter of the total demand, and they sell at present only about half of their total exports to each other. They are, moreover, inclined to think of the United States and, in some degree, the overseas primary producing countries as the great sources of instability in world demand—though they might do well to give some attention to Germany in that connection. At all events, the problem of maintaining a high and steady level of demand is, in the first instance, one which concerns each national economy separately, and, after that, one for the world economy as a whole rather than any regional portion of it. As for the financing of growth, that is a matter in which the west European countries are better able to look after themselves than most; the real problems arise, as we have seen, with countries at a much lower level of development. For some of these, Europe may (and to some extent does) provide both loans and grants, but in general it cannot be the main provider. Once more, this is a world problem, not a regional one.

The next Tasks

We come back, therefore, to the world-wide issues which are the concern of the United Nations and its Specialized Agencies. As we have seen, these have, in large part, already been explored by expert groups reporting to the Economic and Social Council, most notably the groups on Measures for the Economic Development of Underdeveloped Countries (1951), National and International Measures for Full Employment (1949), Measures for International Economic Stability (1951), Commodity Trade and Economic Development

(1953), and A Special United Nations Fund for Economic Development (1953).

In the field of development, the most important recommendation which has emerged from these reports is that for the establishment of a Special United Nations Fund, to provide through politically neutral channels a supply of grants and of long-term loans bearing less than commercial rates of interest. It is for providing the basic services such as education, health services, housing, transport, and power supply, without which particular development projects are not likely to look promising either to the private international lender or to the International Bank, that grants and loans of this character are particularly needed. In the past their place was taken mostly by ordinary government borrowing; it is precisely the inability of the governments of most under-developed countries either to tempt private international lenders or to bear (until development is well under way) the burden of commercial rates of interest on the relatively large borrowings required for catching up with modern standards that creates this need. To satisfy it would require a considerable effort, though one which is not very large in relation to the resources of the advanced countries. The report on Measures for the Economic Development of Under-developed Countries suggests that annual grants or lendings equal to about 1 per cent. of the products of the wealthier countries would serve to promote a substantial, though not by any means a revolutionary rate of progress in the poorer parts of the world. Unfortunately, there has been no move by governments to subscribe even the minimum initial capital of $250 million (perhaps a thirtieth of 1 per cent. of the annual income of the richer countries) with which it was suggested that the Special Fund might make a modest start.

So far as the maintenance of a high and steady level of activity—the prevention of slumps—is concerned, the primary responsibility is bound, as has already been noted, to rest with the governments of the principal countries. If one of these governments allows internal demand in its country to fall off, there is little that the rest of the world can reasonably do to counteract the direct internal effects in the country concerned. The effects on other countries, and the indirect effects on the first country which follow from the effects of its slump on others can, however, in principle be dealt with. The first effect on other countries will normally be a fall in their exports to the country which has the original slump. This, as we saw in the last chapter, will cause slumps in these countries, too (as happened in the United Kingdom in the nineteen-thirties), unless their governments take counter measures, by, for instance, increasing their own expenditure on public works or encouraging private investment. If they do this, they will not only avoid 'importing' the slump (or most of it), they will also save the country where it originated from suffering a second adverse effect through a fall in their demands for its exports.

But to take such counter-measures against a slump when demand for one's country's exports falls off may not be easy—it means, after all, maintaining demand for imports although exports have fallen. Unless exports were greater than imports to start with, this can be done only if there are reserves of foreign currency to draw upon, or if it is possible to borrow—if other countries are willing to let the excess of imports over exports be had on credit. It is by seeing that there are adequate reserves of foreign purchasing power to be drawn upon, or that countries can borrow from abroad to maintain the levels of imports that go with full employment, even though a slump elsewhere may have reduced their exports, that international arrangements can help to contain and reduce depressions. We have seen that the International Monetary Fund is not big enough to do this, but it could be made so, in which case it could go a very long way towards achieving the result just described. The International Bank, too, might, especially if its resources were enlarged, play a part by lending for development schemes preferentially to countries whose exports have been reduced by depression elsewhere. Such measures have been recommended by two of the expert groups mentioned above, but in the absence (so far) of a serious slump no action has been taken. The international economic policies of governments have a strong tendency to resemble those of the man who never thought of going out to buy an umbrella until the rain began, and then could not bring himself to do so for fear of getting wet.

This analogy applies equally to policy with regard to primary commodities. Two of the expert groups have, again, recommended (though with somewhat different emphasis) that more vigorous steps should be taken towards the stabilization of primary commodity prices, though if possible without resorting to restriction of production except temporarily in the event of grave maladjustment. The most obvious way of doing this is through controlling bodies which actually hold stocks of the commodity in question (as the Tin Control does) and so act as 'buffers' to absorb the impact of temporary changes in either demand or supply. To the extent that price fluctuations are due to (and serve to propagate and intensify) fluctuations in demand, this would help also to smooth the course of world income and activity.

Commodity control, moreover, is a topic relevant not only to measures against depression—a subject which some people may be so optimistic (or rash) as to think old-fashioned—but also to measures against inflation, the most widespread of post-war economic diseases. In that it arises largely from the ways in which wages are negotiated and prices of finished products decided in advanced countries, inflation is even more a matter of purely domestic concern, inaccessible to international measures, than depression is. But to a considerable extent it is, as we have seen, a matter also of primary product prices in the world markets, where no single country (except the United States) is usually sufficiently important as a purchaser to exercise much control over events by itself. Widely fluctuating primary product prices promote inflation because their increase stimulates the price-wage spiral in the advanced countries which in turn brings fresh purchasing power to bear in the markets for them; and, moreover, a fall in primary product prices cannot accomplish the all but impossible feat of bringing money wage-rates in advanced countries down. To damp down fluctuation in primary product prices is, therefore, probably the most—if not the only—effective international action that can be taken to stop the upward trend of world prices in general. It is not yet clear, however, that this view is generally accepted, and, even if it were, the political difficulties of comprehensive commodity control would probably prove greater than those in the way of most of the international measures which we have discussed.

These are, in brief, the lines of attack which have been proposed, authoritatively, against the chief malfunctionings of the world economy. Perhaps the main generalization that can be made about them is that they are, in the main, based upon confident and convincing diagnoses of those malfunctionings to a degree which would hardly have seemed credible a generation ago. The present civilization walks among great perils which are partly of its own making, partly rooted in the unchanging frailties of human nature, but at least it need not perish, as it once nearly did, from a failure to understand the mechanics of its own housekeeping.

Index

203